Wooden Spoon
The children's charity of rugby

RUGBYWORLD

25
Years of Rugby
Memories

EDITOR
Ian Robertson

PHOTOGRAPHS
Getty Images

Published in the UK in 2021 by
Lennard Publishing, an imprint of
Lennard Associates Ltd,
Mackerye End,
Harpenden, Herts AL5 5DR
email: orders@lennardqap.co.uk

Distributed by G2 Entertainment
c/o Orca Book Services
160 Eastern Avenue, Milton Park
Abingdon, OX14 4SB

ISBN: 978-1-78281-606-5
ebook: 978-1-78281-607-2

Production editor: Donald Sommerville
Text and cover design: Paul Cooper

The publishers would like to thank Getty Images and their team of top sports photographers for
providing most of the photographs for this book. Dave Rogers deserves a special mention for his
exceptional coverage of rugby throughout the 25 years covered by this book and over many years
before that. The publishers would also like to thank Chris Thau for supplying additional material.

Printed and bound in Italy
by L.E.G.O. S.p.A

CONTENTS

Foreword by HRH The Princess Royal   **5**

1995-2020 Twenty Five Years of Achievement (Wooden Spoon)   **7**

1995-1996 The Arrival of the Wild West (Alastair Hignell)   **11**

1996-1997 A Great Lions Success in South Africa (Sir Ian McGeechan)   **17**

1997-1998 Bath's First Triumph in Europe (Chris Hewett)   **23**

1998-1999 Scotland's Best Win in Paris (Andrew Cotter)   **29**

1999-2000 Australia's Second World Cup Win (Raechelle Inman)   **35**

2000-2001 Leicester: Best at Home and in Europe (David Hands)   **41**

2001-2002 It Was Clive Woodward's Finest Hour (Steve Bale)   **47**

2002-2003 Vernon Pugh, The Game Changer (Chris Thau)   **53**

2003-2004 Dad's Army Win the World Cup (Sir Clive Woodward)   **59**

2004-2005 Wales Grand Slam – Lions Well Beaten (David Stewart)   **65**

2005-2006 Northern Lights Shine at Sale (Stephen Jones)   **71**

2006-2007 'They'll Never Try That Again' (Neale Harvey)   **77**

2007-2008 South Africa and Wales Celebrate (Eddie Butler)   **83**

2008-2009 'If Only': The Tale of the 2009 Lions (Mick Cleary)   **89**

2009-2010 Leicester's Finest Premiership (Paul Bolton)   **95**

2010-2011 The First Major Win for Saracens (Hugh Godwin)   **101**

2011-2012 Lancaster Restores English Pride (Chris Jones)   **107**

2012-2013 The Day The Azzurri beat Les Bleus (John Inverdale)   **113**

2013-2014 Regaining Respect in New Zealand (Chris Foy)   **119**

2014-2015 Glasgow's Miles Better in the Pro12 (Alan Lorimer)   **125**

2015-2016 A Special Irish Win in Cape Town (Peter O'Reilly)   **131**

2016-2017 The Year of Rugby's Ultimate Draw (Miles Harrison)   **137**

2017-2018 St Patrick's Day Well Celebrated (Ruaidhri O'Connor)   **143**

2018-2019 The Finest Calcutta Cup of All (Chris Jones)   **149**

2019-2020 Japan's Wonderful World Cup (Alastair Eykyn)   **155**

Wooden Spoon
The children's charity of rugby

JOIN AS A MEMBER TODAY

and help us through these challenging times

CHOOSE YOUR MEMBERSHIP:

INDIVIDUAL MEMBERSHIP

£5 a month or £50 a year

FAMILY MEMBERSHIP

£8 a month or £90 a year

woodenspoon.org.uk/member

FOREWORD

by HRH THE PRINCESS ROYAL

BUCKINGHAM PALACE

Wooden Spoon's vision, inspired and motivated by its rugby heritage, is to give every child and young person, no matter their background, access to the same opportunities. As an events based charity 2020 has been a very difficult year for us. However in true rugby style, Wooden Spoon has shown great determination and flexibility this year, and has succeeded in distributing emergency funding across the UK and Ireland, to help mitigate the effects of the pandemic on children and young people.

With the tireless support of volunteers and the rugby community, Wooden Spoon has continued its vital work to transform the lives of children and young people with a disability or facing disadvantage. As the children's rugby charity, we use the power of rugby to support a wide range of projects that are not just rugby focused; from sensory rooms, specialist playgrounds and sports activity areas to respite and medical centres and community based projects.

In 2020 Wooden Spoon celebrated 37 years since its formation. In this time, we have distributed in excess of £28 million to more than 1000 projects, helping more than one million children and young people with disabilities or facing disadvantage across the UK and Ireland.

Through adversity we often find opportunity, and I am very pleased to see that the rugby charities are looking at how they can work better together to ensure that more essential funding is being allocated to the frontline, where it is needed more than ever.

As Patron of Wooden Spoon, I would like to thank you for your dedicated interest, enthusiasm and support. This a unique and vibrant charity that will continue to achieve a lot more with your support, changing children's lives through the power of rugby.

Anne

Wooden Spoon
The children's charity of rugby

Twenty Five Years of Achievement

1995–2020

Wooden Spoon, the children's charity of rugby, was founded in 1983. Since then the charity has been committed to enhancing the lives of vulnerable children and young people living in communities across the UK and Ireland. What makes Wooden Spoon unique is that we are a national charity with a local footprint. The majority of our fundraising comes from events organised by our regional volunteers. And every penny raised in their local area is spent on life-changing projects in that location.

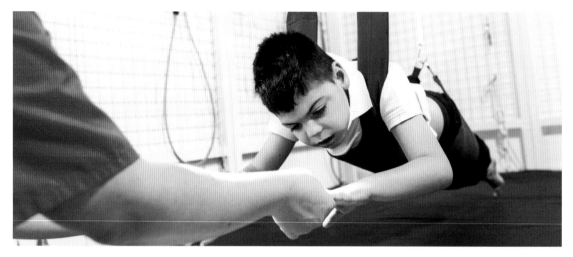

Let's take a look back over the last 25 years of Wooden Spoon
- Children and young people supported: **1,415,000**
- Projects funded: **1,307**
- Money spent on projects: **£27 million**

OUR VISION
Through the power of rugby, every child and young person no matter what their background has access to the same opportunities.
OUR MISSION
To positively transform the lives of children and young people with disabilities or facing disadvantage across the UK and Ireland, through the power of rugby.

ABOVE RIGHT Nigel Timson, President of Wooden Spoon, (left) and Peter Scott, Honorary Life President.

RIGHT Wooden Spoon Ambassadors at the Rugby Ball at the Park Lane Hilton in 2019.

OUR VALUES
Our rugby heritage drives our core values of Passion, Integrity, Teamwork and Fun.
OUR AMBASSADORS
With HRH The Princess Royal as our Patron and a raft of rugby greats among our celebrity
supporters over the last 25 years, the strength of our squad is second-to-none.

Fundraising and rugby world record achievements
In 2015 Wooden Spoon set a new Guinness World Record for playing the northernmost rugby
match in history at the Magnetic North Pole. In 2019 Wooden Spoon set two new Guinness World
Records for playing the highest games of rugby and touch rugby on Mount Everest and added a
third later that year by playing the longest rugby match in history – Wooden Spoon versus the
School of Hard Knocks at Sunbury-on-Thames.

ABOVE LEFT HRH The Princess Royal
with the 2015 Arctic rugby team.

ABOVE RIGHT Raising funds for Wooden
Spoon at the London Marathon.

LEFT Two appropriately dressed teams
at Advanced Base Camp on Mount
Everest in April 2019.

BELOW Referee Graham Allen takes
control of the longest game.

PROJECTS
Examples of our projects:
Education
Wooden Spoon supports HITZ, which is Premiership Rugby's education and employability programme which works with 2,000 14–18 year olds across England every year. Quote by Josh (*pictured below right*): 'My goal after HITZ is to go into construction, which HITZ is helping me with, and to continue playing rugby at New Cross RFC.'

Sensory Rooms and Gardens
The sensory garden at Thornhill Park School in Sunderland provides an area that helps regulate behaviour and meet the sensory requirements of young people with autism.

Health and Wellbeing
Wooden Spoon Scotland funded a larger horse for Riding for the Disabled. The RDA provide therapy, fitness and skill development for people with a range of physical and learning disabilities and autism.

Playground and Outdoor Activities
Wooden Spoon Surrey funded the creation of a wheelchair-accessible raised pond at Nower Wood educational nature reserve. Now, no matter what level of mobility, all visitors, including those with special educational needs and disabilities, are able to explore the amazing diversity of the native pond life.

Specialist Equipment and Facilities
Wooden Spoon Ulster funded two rugby wheelchairs for the Ulster Barbarians. For children without a disability, enabling them to play rugby can often be as simple as buying them a pair of rugby boots and taking them to a local club. For young people with disabilities, a specialist rugby wheelchair can cost £5,000, which can be a massive barrier preventing them from playing.

The Arrival of the Wild West

ALASTAIR HIGNELL

Same old, same old. England retained the Five Nations Championship. Scotland were runners-up, again. Serial winners Bath won the knock-out cup for a tenth time and completed the double with a sixth league championship. Toulouse extended their dominance of the French game with a third consecutive title, while laying an early marker in Europe as inaugural winner of the Heineken Cup.

But the writing was on the wall, and it was written in gold. Rupert Murdoch's victory in the battle of Australian media tycoons had produced an undreamt-of fortune for the South Africa, Australia and New Zealand unions to share, and it was a given that their players would be paid. Three months later – at a meeting of the International Rugby Board in Paris, the Northern Hemisphere unions issued a grudging acceptance of a fait accompli and declared the game open. Pick your metaphor – walls crashing down, resistance crumbling, floodgates opening or, in the words of one of the central figures, Rob Andrew, the arrival of the Wild West – but make no mistake. Rugby would never be the same again.

Few expected the August meeting to go the way it did. The RFU were still righteously pursuing any player suspected of being tainted by the merest brush with the professional code. Scotland and Ireland, where the game was still very much the preserve of the professional middle class, saw little incentive – financial or ethical – to change. In France the relationship between playing and being paid was notoriously elastic. It was slightly tighter in Wales, where the payment of 'boot-money' to amateurs was more than a rumour, but only by a few degrees. The journalists gathering in the French capital expected to report yet another compromise of the type for which rugby union had become notorious. None of them expected to be writing front-page leaders about the complete and utter abandonment of the amateur principle that had defined the game for almost exactly the century after the Northern English clubs' rugby league breakaway in 1895.

BELOW England centre Jeremy Guscott is held by opposite number Nigel Davies of Wales during England's 20–15 win at Twickenham on 3 February 1996.

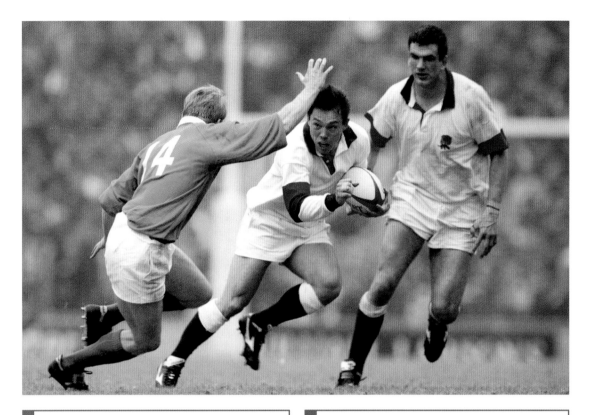

ABOVE England's record try-scorer Rory Underwood looks to swerve outside Simon Geoghan of Ireland during England's 28–15 1996 Five Nations win at Twickenham.

BELOW Gregor Townsend makes a break past Matt Dawson's tackle during the 1996 Calcutta Cup game in Edinburgh. England won the match 18–9.

ABOVE Referee Steve Lander awards Bath a match-winning penalty try in the last seconds of the Pilkington Cup final. Moments later Lander was pushed to the ground by Leicester flanker Neil Back, who was subsequently given a six-month suspension.

Except. As those journalists knew only too well, nothing that emanated from the smoke-filled corridors of the gentlemen's club that in those days went by the name of the International Rugby Board, was ever straightforward. The words were simple enough – the game is now 'open' – but the immediate interpretation of them posed enormous problems.

If it was simple enough in the Southern Hemisphere – the immediate sub-international structure in Australia, South Africa and New Zealand already existed in a form that was easily recognised and remunerated – it was devilishly complicated in the North. Ireland had the structure but lacked the playing numbers, the finance and, initially at least, the inclination to create a sustainable professional sport. Scotland had none of the necessary ingredients, while in Wales, the most successful rugby clubs could not always be found where the money was and inbred parochialism militated against any change to the structure and set-up. Only in England and France did all the ingredients for a successful transition exist but, whereas the game across the Channel barely skipped a beat, English rugby immediately put itself in a self-imposed headlock from which, a quarter of a century later, it is still trying to escape.

It boiled down to cash. The richest and most successful union in the game, with the largest playing base on the planet, could not afford – and was probably reluctant to do so – to set up the sub-international framework that could ensure that its vast off-field wealth could be matched by playing success. The newly rebuilt West and East Stands at Twickenham had left the RFU with a huge debt which it had an instinctive horror of increasing. Instead of putting the top 150 or so players on a central contract – the solution pursued by the Southern Hemisphere unions – the RFU stood back from what many of its backwoodsmen regarded as a holy mess, and in a King Canute-like triumph of hope over logic, imposed a year-long moratorium on professionalism.

The players had gained a fair idea of their worth in the summer months of clandestine meetings with the representatives of the rival broadcasters and they were not inclined to wait. Nor were the home-grown tycoons. Some, bedazzled by the huge sums mentioned in the Murdoch deal, were prepared to speculate that clubs – especially those in prime locations – could be transformed from sleeping giants into cash machines. Others, like Newcastle United owner Sir John Hall, had loftier ambitions. He dreamed of creating a multi-sport super club as Benetton had done in Treviso and he had the resources and sheer bloody-mindedness to do it.

But he was flying blind when it came to costing the operation. His chief lieutenant, Freddy Shepherd, was the vice-chairman of Newcastle United and used to paying footballers' wages. The latter's choice as architect of a playing squad of the required calibre was Wasps and England outside-half Rob Andrew whose day job commanded a London salary and Andrew's choice of a marquee player was Tony Underwood, who was similarly remunerated. Between them they set the benchmark on which all playing salaries either immediate or future have been based – great for the players but not so good for the majority of top clubs who after a quarter of a century of consolidation are still posting a loss.

Bizarrely, Andrew, under a regulation designed for the amateur past and totally unsuitable to the 'Wild West' present, was allowed to continue playing for Wasps while receiving a salary from Newcastle. By the time Wasps had decided that his mind might be on other things, he had signed three senior players in Nick Popplewell, Dean Ryan and the man who was to bring a teenage Jonny Wilkinson along as well – Steve Bates.

Then unknown Exeter punched above their weight by making it to the third round of the Cup, while now obscure Orrell and West Hartlepool – who lost all eighteen league games – just about survived in the top flight.

No English team featured in the inaugural European club competition, the Heineken Cup, leaving the field clear for Toulouse. The French giants played the first match in European Cup history – a comfortable 54–10 victory in

It was hardly surprising that Wasps failed to challenge in either the League or Cup. Both were won by Bath, with arch-rivals Leicester runners-up in each competition, both by the narrowest of margins. The Pilkington Cup Final attracted a world-record 75,000 crowd to Twickenham and featured the controversial dismissal of Leicester flanker Neil Back for pushing referee Steve Lander.

LEFT The Bath team pose after their 16–15 Pilkington Cup win. Andy Robinson and Andy Nicol, on either end of the front row, are among the familiar faces.

TOP Thomas Castaignède scores one of Toulouse's two early tries in the Heineken Cup final, before they eventually won after extra time.

ABOVE Toulouse captain Emile N'Tamack lifts the trophy while scrum-half Philippe Carbonneau (in Cardiff shirt) joins the celebrations of Toulouse's cup-winning success.

Romania against Farul Constanta – and they were rarely tested in their progress to the final, which they won 21–18 in extra time against a Cardiff side playing in their home city.

In the Five Nations, reigning champions England, captained by Will Carling and coached by Geoff Cooke, lost their opening match in France but, scoring only three tries in four matches, still proved too good for the other Home Unions. Scotland, on the back of wins in Ireland and Wales, as well as a home victory over the French, were runners-up. Ireland scored four tries against Wales but only one other in open play as they finished last. In a largely unmemorable competition, dominated by the boot, England outside-half Paul Grayson kicked a record 64 points.

By the end of the season Grayson and all his England team-mates had signed professional contracts and the next batch of millionaire investors were on their way. Nigel Wray had started to wield his hefty chequebook on behalf of Saracens, while copper trader Ashley Levett had taken an extraordinary gamble on third division Richmond, and Formula One boss Tom Walkinshaw was being courted by Gloucester.

And rugby league stars were on their way back. Only months before the Paris meeting , the RFU had banned a Cambridge University amateur because he had previously played rugby league. Now it had no choice but to welcome those that it once deemed pariahs. By the end of the season former Wales rugby union internationals Scott Quinnell and Allan Bateman had quit the thirteen-man code to hitch up with Richmond, while Rob Andrew had recruited Alan Tait, once of Scotland, and John Bentley, once of England. With them they brought the lived experience of professional sport.

The message was two-way and couldn't have been clearer. Rugby Union, at a stroke, could offer comparable wages and vastly greater opportunities for international recognition. The returnees, soon to be followed by some, like Jason Robinson and Gary Connolly, who had never tried the union code, would show exactly what it meant to be a professional, rugby-playing athlete. Rugby at the end of the 1995/96 season might have looked the same as it had done twelve months earlier, but no one close to it was in any doubt.

This was a whole new ball game.

A Great Lions Success in South Africa

SIR IAN McGEECHAN

I t is safe to say that the 1996/97 season is one that I will never forget, so many incredible things happened in relation to that year's Lions' tour. What remains with me to this day is the recollection of the number of decisions and actions that were done differently than before.

It started with a unique selection process coming out of lessons learned from the two previous Lions tours – we agreed that Fran Cotton, as manager, myself and Jim Telfer would select the squad. If we were going to fail it would be with the players of our choice, not by committee, as had occurred in 1993. With us were four 'player observers', one from each country – Peter Rossborough (England), Derek Quinnell (Wales), Donal Lenihan (Ireland) and Ian Laurie (Scotland).

I had had the opportunity during the previous summer to visit South Africa and share time and thoughts with the All Blacks whilst they were on tour. Coach John Hart and his players could not have been more helpful. We spoke about the challenges of playing a Test series in South Africa. Significantly, that 1996 tour was the first ever New Zealand series win in South Africa.

PREVIOUS PAGE Sir Ian McGeechan, on tour with the Lions in 1997.

I watched the Test matches, listened, asked questions and learned. When I returned I had a clear picture in my mind of the rugby we would need to be prepared to play if we were to have a chance of winning the series. I put together a twenty-page report which included my idea of the requirements needed in every position, and, most importantly, the type of player who would be prepared to respond to that approach.

As a group of seven, we watched and compared every international player and international squad player in each position and put them on a scale against the requirements written down. Our 1997 Lions had to have the confidence to play and respond to the actions of each other in any given situation, to be as good without the ball as they were with it and, most of all, to be prepared to approach and play the game differently: work as 'teams within the team'.

After many hours of deliberation and discussions, Fran, Jim and I believed we had a group of players who would be prepared to be different and create an identity with characteristics totally unfamiliar to those in the Southern Hemisphere. As I said to them on our very first day together, 'We must aim to put a marker down in South Africa about the way we can play our rugby.'

Why have I started with this? Because, looking back, if we had not challenged ourselves to think differently from the outset as a management, we would have fallen short. People create the environment, the environment creates the atmosphere, the atmosphere puts smiles on faces. If you enjoy being there you will find ways of performing when it matters to make the difference.

ABOVE With a quick break following a powerful scrum, Matt Dawson touches down for the Lions during the First Test in Cape Town, 21 June 1997. The Lions sealed a 16–25 victory with two late tries.

LEFT 28 June 1997: former rugby league professional John Bentley of the Lions tackles Pieter Rossouw of South Africa during the Second Test, at Kings Park, Durban. The Lions won 15–18 and secured the series win.

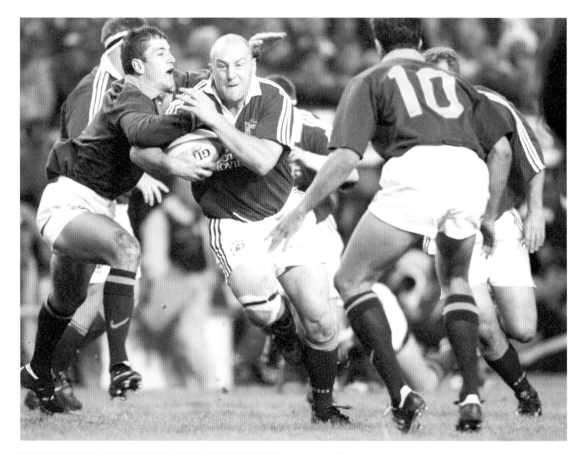

ABOVE Lions hooker Keith Wood is tackled by the Springbok scrum-half, the late Joost van der Westhuizen, during the First Test.

Looking back, that preparation and our first week together in Weybridge still give me a very special feeling. Finishing the week with the players creating and agreeing their own 'Lions Laws' led to a relaxed evening together over a few beers in a Weybridge pub.

As the tour unfolded the pleasing memory was the growing collective strength within the group and the environment the players were ultimately creating. I have never seen Jim Telfer smile as much and relax. He enjoyed himself and the challenge because he knew he was coaching, not just good rugby players, but good men. Men he could trust.

At training the players showed the commitment to play with ball in hand at high pace, to know there would always be a support runner behind them if they were carrying the ball, a 'shotgun' player who would be there to link away from contact. They got used to grouping in fours and fives in phase play as attack – link – support teams, consistently giving us a secondary attack line.

> In pure rugby terms the games leading up to the First Test and the Orange Free State game produced some incredible rugby – by the whole squad. In my head I always carried the picture of the perfect game – we got very close to it during those times.

Watching this game evolve in training was extremely enjoyable and satisfying, and with each game played it was emerging more and more consistently through the eighty minutes. We had a habit of adding significant points in the last twenty minutes of games and a belief to keep playing to achieve this.

What impressed and surprised me was the reaction I received from the players when I tried to change some of the practices where support running was key. I wanted to freshen some things up. 'Don't change them' came

ABOVE Jeremy Guscott celebrates his match-winning drop goal in the Second Test in Durban. The Kings Park scoreboard has not yet changed to display the Lions' new 18–15 lead.

the response, 'If we don't concentrate we can't do them, they keep us honest, they challenge us.' So the 2 *vs* 1 + 1, the 3 *vs* 2 + 1, and so on stayed. As did our Tuesday defence day. A happy coaching memory, because I was getting feedback from the players. As a coach you need that, it inspires. Here was a collective intelligence, commitment and responsibility that Jim and I appreciated.

Analysis had become an important part of our process and Andy Keast was responsible for it, although a coach in his own right. As part of that I had worked with Keith Lyons at the Centre for Notational Analysis in Cardiff. He was faxing out data two or three times a week, particularly on phase time, speed of ball, and time with and without the ball at different points in the game.

Before the First Test I asked Keith if he would put together a video of how we were looking in his eyes 6,000 miles away. The video arrived on the Friday morning before the Test match in Cape Town. At the end of our team meeting in the evening I put the tape on for the players and told them it was a reflection on how our game was being viewed back home. What followed was twelve minutes of rugby, put to music, but what was significant was that in the first six minutes we did not have the ball; the second six minutes showed our phase attacks with the support. Keith had added a note – 'What is impressive is how good the team is when it does not have the ball; with the ball, how good the support lines are.' When I pressed the stop button after the first showing – silence.

Here was a tape showing our rugby in a different shape, and in those twelve minutes every player was shown. This was their game. During the evening I went back into the team room on a number of occasions, and each time the tape was being played, and replayed. A special environment was emerging.

The next day we surprised South Africa in the scrum, we were consistent in support and not afraid to play when creating the opportunity – outstandingly reflected in Matt Dawson's try, coming off a superb scrum. And, without the ball, we gave them no space. We once again had a strong last twenty minutes. A First Test match won.

We went out for a meal after the game quite late because of the kick-off time. Fran had organised a meal out at a Mexican restaurant – full of supporters and waitresses serving cocktails from hip flasks! On the way there Martin Johnson stood up in the coach and reminded the Test team that training was at 9.00 the next morning (Sunday) and they were all needed to hold tackle shields for the team playing Orange Free State on Tuesday evening. He also said that the team which wins only one Test match will not be remembered.

TOP (*Left to right*) Alan Tait, Matt Dawson and Neil Jenkins of the British Lions celebrate the First Test win over South Africa. Dawson and Jenkins started in all three Tests of the tour; Tait scored a last-minute try in the First Test and also started in the Second, but was injured for the final match.

ABOVE A bloody Adrian Garvey of South Africa after the Third Test, at Ellis Park, Johannesburg. South Africa won 35–16 but the Lions had already clinched the series. Despite his battered appearance Garvey, who came on as a replacement, had only played the last twenty minutes of the match.

Next morning all the players were present and on the coach, but not the TV crew, who had slept in! We trained well and moved on to Durban.

Another abiding memory is of the Second Test in Durban with Jim and I sat in the stand surrounded by Springbok supporters – there was no coaches' box then!

After a huge defensive effort, countering wave after wave of Springbok attacks, we gradually controlled more possession and with Neil Jenkins's goal-kicking keeping us in the game we broke out of our own half and produced three special minutes of rugby in which different players took responsibility to turn over a ball and play – Jerry Guscott winning a ruck turn-over, Keith Wood kicking long from scrum-half and forcing a line-out in South Africa's 22. A good line-out win and drive, Gregor Townsend running straight and hard for the try line at the heart of South Africa's defence, ruck won, Matt Dawson to Jerry Guscott, drop-goal, 15–18 with three minutes to play.

Jim, who had been having serious banter with the South Africans around us, whispered, but didn't look at me, 'Three minutes from glory, three minutes from glory, come on boys.' What followed was the longest three minutes of my rugby life. I had my heart in my mouth when Neil Jenkins kicked a 22 drop-out directly into touch, then exhilaration, total joy and relief when the final whistle was blown. The end of two incredible, but very different Test matches.

Later that evening Jim, myself and Judy, my wife, had a quiet but hugely enjoyable meal together, just taking in everything that had happened, and a nice bottle of red wine compliments of the hotel.

Some players had a party and slept on the beach, before making it back to the hotel for breakfast – each to his own! We left the hotel to an ovation from the hundreds of Lions fans who had congregated in the foyer and outside. The great phenomenon, the Lions and their support, nothing quite like it. Oh, and I had had a haircut! 1997 – Special.

Bath's First Triumph in Europe

CHRIS HEWETT

It is all well and good a team being ahead of the competition – trophy-winning sides are, by definition, better than their immediate rivals – but true champions must also be ahead of their time. When Bath became the first English club to lay hands on the Heineken Cup by defeating the holders Brive on a winter's afternoon in 1998, they cashed in on an investment stretching back a decade – years during which they refused to settle for a fine yesterday and set their sights on a bolder, more adventurous tomorrow.

That 'tomorrow' was based around regular challenges against the best sides on the European mainland. Bath won their first domestic league title in 1988/89, under the captaincy of Stuart Barnes, but in the grand scheme of things, one match was more significant than the rest. And it didn't involve Leicester or Wasps or Bristol, still less the likes of Clifton or Cheltenham or the Public School Wanderers, or any of the other lower-grade opponents who would fade from the wider public view with the onset of professionalism.

BELOW Matthew Lloyd of Pontypridd (*left*) hands off David Venditti of Brive in the Heineken Cup quarter-final play-off, the third meeting between the two teams in that season's tournament. Brive won this match, fortunately less controversial than their first encounter, 25–20.

The game in question was against Toulouse, who pitched up at the Recreation Ground on Halloween weekend in 1988 and spooked their hosts with a try by the sublime Test centre Didier Codorniou. The Frenchmen, coached by Pierre Villepreux, no less, left

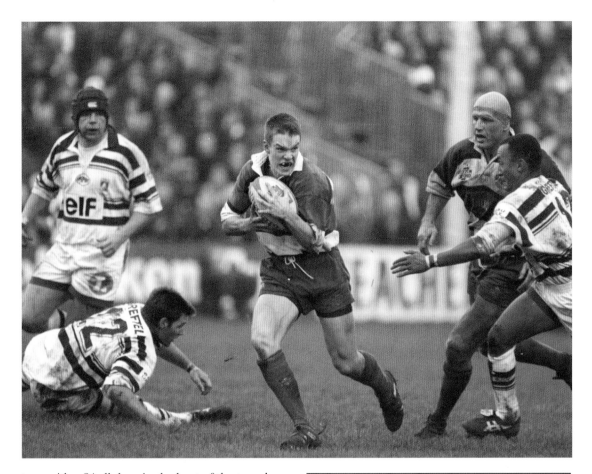

town with a 24-all draw in the boot of the team bus – an outcome that provoked an outpouring of humility from the Bath boss Jack Rowell, who, it is fair to suggest, was not overly familiar with the emotion. 'It was tremendous rugby and I'm sure we learned a lot from it,' he said when quizzed on events.

Bath would continue along the learning pathway, hosting Steaua Bucharest and Toulon the following season and participating in the Toulouse centenary tournament at the back end of 1990. This trailblazing streak was not popular with the more die-hard conservatives on the management committee – there was a fearful internal row when Rowell and his senior lieutenants organised a home game against a Romanian XV for the same weekend as a long-planned visit to Pontypool – but the outward-looking approach had taken root amongst the people who really mattered: the coaches and the players.

Plenty happened, some of it very dark, over the following few seasons of rugby upheaval, both to the sport in general and to Bath in particular. But the establishment of European-wide tournament rugby in the form of the Heineken Cup was an unalloyed positive. The West Countrymen were more enthusiastic about it than anyone, given their history as pioneers, and they set their sights on winning the competition at the first attempt, in 1996/97.

Which emphatically didn't happen. Badly beaten at Pontypridd in the pool stage, they lumbered themselves with a quarter-final on the road and duly lost to Cardiff on a broodingly intense afternoon at the Arms Park, having left out the England full-back Jon Callard and taken the field without a specialist goal-kicker. 'I have no regrets,' said the Bath director of rugby, John Hall. To which his counterpart, Terry Holmes, responded: 'I wouldn't even contemplate going into a game like that without a recognised kicker.' Only one of them was right, and he spoke with a Welsh accent.

Callard was very much on the field when Bath finally realised their dearest ambition a year later than planned, and ironically enough, it was he who did the realising, scoring every last one of his side's points – a

try, a conversion, four penalties – in the 19–18 victory over Brive at the beautiful Stade Lescure in Bordeaux. But this is not the full story. Or even half the story.

What made it really interesting at first was the presence of Pontypridd in the same group, especially when the Welshmen ventured across the water (the Channel, not the Severn) and became embroiled in the mother and father of dust-ups – a prolonged piece of fistic theatre staged in two acts, the first of them on the pitch and the second in Le Bar Toulzac, a small watering hole in the middle of town where the two teams were reacquainted after the match, with consequences so dire that the place might have been renamed Le Bar Tooled-Up.

There was serious talk of the return fixture being scrapped, but it went ahead without incident and ended in a draw, which was probably as well. The two sides even contrived to meet again, in a quarter-final play-off tie back in Brive. That, too, was a close-run

LEFT Sebastien Carrat of Brive celebrates scoring the winning try during the Heineken Cup semi-final at the Stade Toulousain, Toulouse, 21 December 1997.

BELOW Second-row Fabien Pelous of Toulouse finds no way through the Brive defence during the semi-final. This was Pelous's first season with the club and he would go on to be France's most capped player of all time, captaining his country on many occasions.

ABOVE Nigel Redman of Bath (*centre*) is wrapped up by the Pau defence during the Heineken semi-final at the Recreation Ground. Bath went on to win 20–14.

thing, the Frenchmen eventually prevailing by five points. From Bath's perspective, this was gold dust. Instead of being the talk of the tournament, they were a sideshow act with room to breathe and time to plan. Thanks to their opponents' draw at Sardis Road, they topped the pool by a point and went straight into the last eight with home advantage.

Cardiff, of all people, were the quarter-final visitors and were duly dealt with by an 11-point margin. Bath also had a little too much for Pau in the last four, much to the relief of all at the Rec. If Pau were hardly the flashiest of teams, they had spanked Leicester 35–18 in the previous round and were clearly nobody's fools.

But taking on the reigning champions in France – champions who had come through the fires of the Pontypridd conflagration and gone on to beat Bath on home soil, win a quarter-final tie at Wasps and prevail over a lavishly-equipped

> The two finalists had been drawn in the same pool for the round-robin stage, which was intriguing enough: the low-profile over-achievers from the Corrèze, who had blindsided everyone in putting four tries past a heavily favoured Leicester side in the previous season's showpiece, together with the Europhiles-in-chief from Somerset, who had full internationals coming out of their cauliflower ears.

Toulouse outfit in the semis – would be '*une autre paire de manches*'. Brive had strengthened since winning the title the year before: they now boasted the brilliant Olivier Magne in the back row and the accomplished Argentinian international Lisandro Arbizu as playmaker-in-chief. Everyone thought they would win, including

ABOVE Victor Ubogu of Bath (with ball) knocks aside Christophe Lamaison of Brive during the European Cup final at the Stade Lescure, Bordeaux.

the Bath supporters who filled Bordeaux on match weekend.

Truth be told, the contest was played out in drab shades of grey, wholly at odds with the glorious Technicolor generated by the two tribes of spectators, and there were times when it seemed that Christophe Lamaison's accuracy from the kicking tee would allow Brive to retain the trophy with something to spare.

When the Scottish referee Jim Fleming brought things to a conclusion at long, long last, there was an air of bewilderment in the stands. Then the bedlam began, and by the time they had exhausted the many drinking options on offer in the centre of town, the Bath supporters had forgotten the agonies of the match. 'Never in doubt,' they sang in boozy unison. Yeah. Right.

Yet Bath refused to buckle. There was a seven-scrum goal-line stand in which the front row of Dave Hilton, Mark Regan and Victor Ubogu went everywhere except backwards in successfully defending their honour. There was a tap-tackle by Ieaun Evans that prevented the extremely rapid Sebastian Carrat from putting the contest to bed.

And then there was Callard, picked ahead of the first-choice England full-back Matt Perry because no one trusted Mike Catt to kick the goals from outside-half. 'Mr Stroppy', as he had long been known, was positively serene when it mattered, not least in putting himself on the shoulder of Jeremy Guscott for the only try of the afternoon – a score that reduced the Brive lead to two points – and then nailing the most pressurised of penalties four minutes into injury time.

Not that it ended there. How could it, after such a campaign? Lamaison, usually so strong at these moments, butchered a penalty shot of his own as the clock continued to tick. Then Arbizu missed by inches with a drop-goal attempt. But that was the last chance gone.

Scotland's Best Win in Paris

ANDREW COTTER

They were almost all there, gathered in the downstairs dining room of some well turned-out Edinburgh establishment. There to raise money for Tom Smith and Doddie Weir and also to remember . . . two decades on.

At one table was Doddie himself, alongside Gary Armstrong, Alan Tait and Gregor Townsend. Kenny Logan was holding court as ever. Among the others were the Leslie brothers, Stuart Grimes, Peter Walton, Paul Burnell and Eric Peters. Glenn Metcalfe had even flown in from New Zealand. And Jim Telfer was close by, appearing as a more benign incarnation of the deity, but still somehow terrifying them all.

This was a reunion of Scotland's claiming of the last ever Five Nations Championship in 1999 and, as the drink flowed, the stories were told and the memories came flooding back.

You see, to realise why that year was so special to Scotland, you have to understand the context.

In the eighties and early nineties Scotland had, by and large, been good. Very good. A Grand Slam in 1984, a wonderful new wave of talent appearing in 1986, another slam in 1990, then close to beating the All Blacks in Auckland and within a whisker of a World Cup final. Even in the mid-nineties there were Grand Slam dreams which only dissipated with final-game defeats to England.

Then came the revolution.

The myriad reasons why the game turning professional was not good for Scotland are too numerous to detail here, but by the late nineties, Scotland's national team was suffering. They were spared wooden spoons in '97 and '98 only by Ireland, who continued to bump along the bottom (yet were about to enter the greatest period in their history). There was also the painful humiliation of the heaviest-ever defeat for the national team – conceding 68 points at home against South Africa. As the Springboks strolled in their tenth try and the final whistle went, it looked like just what it was – a mismatched contest between amateur and professional eras.

Scottish rugby was lurching towards the new millennium and that was why 1999 was so special. Because it was so unexpected.

Part of it might have been down to the fact that Jim Telfer stepped in as head coach (although Richie Dixon actually had a decent record). More likely it was due to the bedding in of some very special players – Alan Tait had returned from rugby

LEFT Scott Murray of Scotland wins a line-out against Ireland in the 30–13 win at Murrayfield, 20 March 1999.

league and the far reaches of the Scottish diaspora were mined for rich talents. The Leslie brothers – centre John and flanker Martin – along with full-back Glenn Metcalfe and wing Shaun Longstaff had arrived from New Zealand.

There were also those who had more tenuous connections but were no less important figures – another flanker Budge Pountney qualified either through a grandmother from the Channel Islands or possibly because he had once watched an episode of *Bergerac*. (Channel Islanders could evidently pick their own Home Nation.) Yet, however these players got the call, they all came together and something clicked.

And it did so right at the start of that Championship – John Leslie scoring a try within nine seconds of the whistle in Scotland's opening game against Wales. There was also one piece of fortune which shaped that Scottish side – ill-fortune for one player, Duncan Hodge, as he broke his leg in that game. So, early in the second-half, Gregor Townsend had to move from centre to fly-half with Alan Tait coming off the bench. The Townsend–Tait–Leslie midfield was formed and became, with Metcalfe at full-back, one of the best attacking forces ever to sport the thistle.

Indeed, it was a Championship which was bookended by drama. That opening game was crucial and, of course, the final game of the Championship – between Wales and England – when Scott Gibbs skipped and stepped his way to the try-line at Wembley (Wales's home ground while work went on in the Millennium Stadium) – was when the title actually went to Scotland. But the game which summed up Scotland's glorious campaign happened the day before, in Paris.

I watched from afar – I was working in local radio in Edinburgh and could only glance up at the television in the studio while delivering updates on something like Hearts against St Johnstone, which the sports editor felt was more important. Yet even he conceded that something of note was occurring as the first half went on, for it was arguably the greatest half of rugby that Scotland have ever played (although the second half of the Calcutta Cup at Twickenham in 2019 would also present a fairly strong case).

But back in April 1999, we watched as Scotland scored first. This in itself was impressive, against France who had completed Grand Slams in '97 and '98, the same France who had scored a combined 98 points in their two previous romps against Scotland.

Then disbelief and celebration increased as try after try followed. Five tries . . . in just twenty minutes . . . By this point even the afternoon DJ, a football die-hard who regularly dismissed 'egg-chasing', was looking interested. 'This is pretty good isn't it?'

'Yes . . . yes it is,' I assured him.

ABOVE Gregor Townsend of Scotland slips a short pass to John Leslie in the 22–36 win in Paris, 10 April 1999.

ABOVE Scrum-half Gary Armstrong links with the backs during the remarkable win against France.

ABOVE The Leslie brothers (John, *left*) with the Five Nations Trophy at the Murrayfield celebration the day after the Wembley game.

ABOVE Scott Gibbs scores the try that sealed it for Scotland, denying England the Grand Slam, at Wembley of all places.

Outside the studio I could see a news reporter – a chap called Ramsay Jones, who went on to be fairly prominent in the Scottish government – running around, arms outstretched in celebration as the fourth and fifth tries went in. Gregor Townsend completed his own personal sweep of scoring in every game of the tournament. It was, as he would describe it years later, 'my favourite day in a Scotland jersey'.

Mine, too, as the fan I still was. These were in broadcasting days before I commentated, before I had to maintain a neutrality and could still feel like a supporter. Besides, I worked for a station called Scot FM and maintaining an objective distance was not necessarily encouraged. And this was a day when belief in Scottish rugby and that joy of being a fan returned. Yes, there are some in the Scottish rugby community who still, in quieter moments of reflection, rue the missed opportunity at Twickenham – a game when Alan Tait had inspired, but kicks were missed, which meant a 24–21 defeat, and a possible Grand Slam was lost.

Far more, though, prefer to think of that first half in Paris when the tries flowed on the sunlit field of the Stade de France and, for a while, all was right with the Scottish rugby world. With the win in 1999 it seemed as if Scotland could thrive and succeed once more. The rugby played was fast and entertaining, it was springtime in Paris, the dark days were behind us and this was the rebirth of the game in Scotland.

Of course, anybody who took the trouble to scratch lightly at the glistening veneer would have realised that it was a thin polish to cover all sorts of problems. Scottish rugby was still ill-prepared for the professional world and the next fifteen years would demonstrate that quite clearly.

Yet there is contentment in not peering too far into the future and none of that mattered at the hastily-organised celebration at Murrayfield on the Monday, where 10,000 supporters turned up to welcome the unexpected prize of the last Five Nations trophy. True, the win in France and the title which followed proved not to be the positive start of the professional era – rather the glorious last hurrah of the amateur one. But that only seems to make them even more special.

That's why 1999 will always be fondly remembered. And why that team – a curious blend of personalities and talents – would still travel from far and wide to gather together in Edinburgh two decades later. To remember and reminisce. For Scottish rugby, that season was the final flickering of a light which would not be seen again for some time.

But in 1999, when it burned its last, it was beautiful.

Australia's Second World Cup Win

RAECHELLE INMAN

1999 • 6-9 • 2007 • 2000

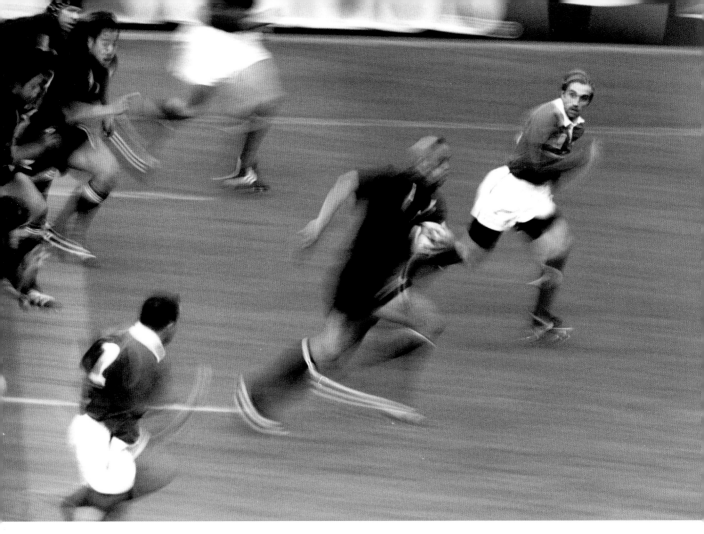

The fourth Rugby World Cup was blessed with a unique buzz and energy, it had a carnival atmosphere. Indeed, it was similar to the magical ambience of the Olympics in Sydney the following year. This atmosphere was at a spectacular high for the All Blacks versus France semi-final at Twickenham. Somehow, when something unexpected happens, especially when it involves an underdog rising to brilliance, it supercharges the energy.

That was how I found myself chanting 'Allez Les Bleus' from the press box at Twickenham in late October 1999.

France, ahhhh, the nation has a special place in my heart. I love the passion for life, the style, the food, the wine, the beauty, the way the French are decisive and don't worry so much about what others think. I love the French rugby jersey and those red socks, oh my goodness – they look incredible! As for their team, the unpredictability of the French is so exciting. They run hot and cold. One minute the French are decidedly average – the next they lift and play out of their skins. They can be world-beaters, on any day. Every Aussie rugby fan remembers the semi-final of the first World Cup in 1987 when Serge Blanco dashed the hopes of the home side, crossing the line in the dying minutes of the game at Concord Oval in Sydney – about 99 per cent of the crowd was stunned into silence whilst about 150 French supporters in the East Stand went nuts. What a day, and what a moment. Unforgettable.

New Zealand is like an extension of Australia in many ways – we are geographically close, we fought wars together, there is so much history in the spirit of the ANZACs. But when it comes to rugby the Kiwis are our arch-rivals, so '*allez Les Bleus*' was being screamed by every green-and-gold-wearing Australian rugby fan, and frankly by anyone who wasn't a New Zealander, at Twickenham that day.

ABOVE Jonah Lomu of New Zealand in full flow during the semi-final against France.

The 1999 event was the first World Cup held in the sport's professional era. That year the All Blacks seemed to be so far ahead of the rest of the game. They had world rugby's biggest weapon – Jonah Lomu. He

ABOVE Number 8 Abdel Benazzi of France hands off Jeff Wilson of New Zealand during the dramatic semi-final.

was at his peak, an absolute freak – a mould breaker. Power, size and speed combined to make him unstoppable. Fast as a sprinter, strong as a wrestler, he weighed 120 kilograms and was just shy of two metres tall, yet he was a gentle giant, humble and softly spoken off the field. In addition to the prolific winger, the Kiwi backline in '99 also boasted Andrew Mehrtens, Christian Cullen, Tana Umaga and Jeff Wilson. Mehrtens and Cullen were two of my favourite players to interview, down to earth, good guys. In 1999 it seemed they were a sure thing to make the final.

But there was a monkey on the back of the All Blacks – there was a fair bit of talk even back then about the New Zealanders being World Cup 'chokers'. After winning in the inaugural World Cup in 1987, they hadn't been able to repeat their success (and wouldn't until 2011).

The semi-final started with an early try for Christophe Lamaison; it was a small flicker of French hope. But New Zealand accelerated into the lead with Lomu bagging a double to raise his tally in World Cup semi-finals to six tries in two appearances. All was going to script as New Zealand ran up a 24–10 lead.

But two drop-goals from Lamaison changed the momentum of the game. Lamaison booted two more quick penalties and soon after half-back Fabien Galthié, kicked an up-and-under down the left touchline. Diminutive winger Christophe Dominici stormed after it and raced around Mehrtens to score.

All of a sudden, and quite inexplicably, France were in the lead.

This drive continued; Lamaison was on fire, he chipped into the arms of Richard Dourthe, who crossed the line for another five-pointer. Before the dust settled France had scored 33 points without reply. Although New Zealand full-back Jeff Wilson answered with a try late in the game for the All Blacks, 'Les Bleus' held on for an unbelievable 43–31 victory. The hopes of New Zealand were crushed completely and unexpectedly by the most French of French performances. And it was beautiful to watch.

I happened to wear a beautiful coat and a beret to that semi-final at Twickenham. It seemed fitting that I was dressed like a French woman. Back in those days I was the only female journalist primarily covering rugby, and my presence in the commentary team on Australian radio was most unusual. I was twenty-three years old and the World Cup was my third international rugby tour. I worked across TV, radio and print. To be certain I

understood the technical aspects of the game I had even asked a referee to give me lessons about the intricate nature of the laws of rugby to ensure I maintained high levels of credibility. I found out years later that most of the experienced, much older male journalists didn't understand some of the technical rules.

One of my favourite memories of this time was the richness, rawness and honesty in the interviews, even the press conferences. Open professionalism had been introduced three years prior, but rugby was still in transition. Whilst the game itself was starting to show improvements with enhanced skills developing and more analytics around tactics, the attitudes, culture and the 'vibe' surrounding the game still maintained some of the freshness, candour and fun of the amateur times. Teams were not being overly protected; they were accessible and not media-trained within an inch of their lives, which made for some good, honest commentary and authenticity. It wasn't contrived or manufactured – it was real.

The passion to represent one's country was enough. The money didn't seem to count as much as the honour, seemingly very different to the sports-science- and data-driven game that appears visibly more soulless today.

RIGHT Owen Finegan heads for the try line to round out Australia's triumph.

After the press conferences during the World Cup, at one of the most impressive Welsh hotels, I would wander across the road to the pub, take out my laptop, order a glass of wine, edit my video and audio files and transfer them for live posting online and for them to be played on radio in Australia. This was the start of the internet and instant content. I was the only journalist handling my own files this way. Back in those days I was a first mover; my colleagues would laugh now to hear I was once so tech savvy.

The nineties were a significant decade for me. I finished high school. I completed an economics degree. And I embarked on a career as a sports journalist. Blockbuster movies like *Jerry Maguire, Austin Powers, Clueless* and *The Titanic* were released. The Harry Potter franchise launched. American TV shows such as *Beverly Hills 90210* and *Melrose Place* were popular. Oasis, Madonna, Nirvana, Ricky Martin and the Spice Girls pumped out hit songs.

In 1999 there was a significant anxiety about Y2K, the computer bug that was feared would cause extensive havoc to worldwide programs and systems as the year changed to 2000. But you wouldn't have known it in Cardiff during the World Cup, even though it was only two months before the end of 1999.

The Millennium Stadium was sensational for the opening ceremony. I recall Shirley Bassey belting out the uplifting theme song of the tournament, 'The World in Union'. She did Wales proud and so did the local crowd in the stadium singing the most divine Welsh hymns and arias with gusto. That anthem still holds up well and brings rugby fans together more than twenty years later.

The final also had a buzz about it. For an Aussie it was particularly special that the Wallabies made the final. Many of the players were of a similar age to me so I felt like I was growing up with them. The team, the coach Rod Macqueen, the support staff, such as John Best, the team doctor, were all so lovely to me. So inclusive. I felt like I was part of the inner sanctum. I doubt that would happen now as teams tend to be much more protected and seem more wary of the media. With digital and social media saturation maybe the cautious approach is understandable.

Australia had only just beaten South Africa in the other semi-final, an extremely close and exciting match-up. Tim Horan had played an incredible game. Well into injury time with the score gridlocked at 21-all, from 45 metres out Stephen Larkham rose to hero status with his extraordinary penalty to seal a coveted spot in the final for the Wallabies.

The Australian side sustained excellence throughout this tournament and that earned them the right to be World Champions. John Eales, Tim Horan and Matt Burke were absolutely world class throughout the competition.

Australia had expected to be facing New Zealand in the final so had to quickly re-work their game plan to take on France. The two finalists were ball-running teams and there was some free-flowing running rugby and a lack of structure, but South African referee André Watson pulled up play way too often and the game was ruled by penalties. It became a stop–start affair. After their dazzling effort in the semi-final the French were flat, so the game wasn't quite the spectacle everyone had hoped for. Semis are often better games than finals.

The Australian defence was strong; they had conceded just one try all tournament and kept another clean sheet in the final.

Les Blues tried on their eye-gouging and testicle-grabbing dirty tactics but to no avail. After warnings from the New Zealand team management after their semi-final loss regarding French foul play, the Wallabies had

ABOVE Australia captain John Eales, with arms aloft, celebrates Owen Finegan's clinching try in the final.

decided to threaten to walk off if the French played too dirty. After a few incidents, including Australian winger Joe Roff copping a finger in his eye, Eales can be heard making a point over the referee's microphone: 'I fear for my team's safety. If this continues, we will leave the field.'

Having played their thriller the week prior, France looked lacklustre, particularly in the second half and the Wallabies stepped up their attack. One of the Wallabies' star speedsters, Ben Tune, crossed in the corner, his try was converted by Burke and Australia were ahead 28–12 with fifteen minutes to go.

In the final stages there was a textbook line-out on the France 10-metre line. An easy win for Eales from the throw in, tapped neatly to Gregan. A classic Brumbies cheeky inside flick pass from Gregan found Owen Finegan, who had looped around and ran onto the ball, breaking through. The Gregan pass was perfectly timed. The replacement flanker seemed to be looking around for someone to give the ball to and eventually realised he had to crash over himself, and he did, for the try that secured the match, and the title of World Champions. And 'Melon,' as he was known, couldn't believe his luck, it was priceless, his face told the story – he was in disbelief and was ecstatic simultaneously.

Of course, that move had started with John Eales, one of the most complete players ever to play the game; his nickname was appropriately 'Nobody', simply because 'nobody's perfect'. Eales, the captain stood tall, towering above the Queen when he graciously received the William Webb Ellis trophy from her in the same week that Australians had voted in a referendum to keep the British monarch as Australia's head of state.

After Australia won the game 35–12 Eales said: 'When Ben Tune scored that try, yeah, it was looking pretty good, but we still couldn't be sure, because of what we'd seen the French do the week before. But when Owen Finegan ran in his try, we knew that was it. And it's pretty rare in a major sporting event that you can almost relax, like, you don't turn off, but you can almost relax. You know you've won it and we really just enjoyed the last five or ten minutes of that game, like I've never enjoyed a game of football I think.'

And I know exactly how he felt, it wasn't the prettiest of games, but it was an exceptional result, and it was well-deserved. My Wallabies had won the World Cup, and it was a cracking tournament. That is why 1999 is my favourite year for world rugby.

Leicester: Best at Home and in Europe

DAVID HANDS

This was a year that, in England, kept on giving. At least, it did if you think in terms of a six-month calendar and the stature reached by the country's leading players during that period. In four matches, Clive Woodward's England played their most relaxed attacking rugby of his tenure as coach and eight of his team started in the British and Irish Lions XV which put Australia to the sword in Brisbane at the end of June.

Thereafter it all went pear-shaped. The Lions lost the remaining two tests, in controversial circumstances, and England's anticipated Grand Slam went west when they lost to Ireland in the Six Nations match postponed for six months because of the foot-and-mouth outbreak that year. But in those first four games, they scored tries for fun: six against Wales, ten against Italy, six against Scotland and six more against France, six of those twenty-eight falling to Will Greenwood.

But if English rugby followers wanted icing on their cake and a cherry on top as spring turned into summer, Leicester gave it to them when they became the third English club – after Bath and Northampton – to win the Heineken Cup. Here an interest should be declared: having spent seven years working for the *Leicester Mercury* and written the centenary history of the Tigers, I had more than a passing knowledge of, and enthusiasm for, the club which was hard to live down, even after moving away from the area.

That they became the most successful club of the early professional era is beyond dispute, even for those who persisted (erroneously) in viewing them as one-dimensional. Tigers had, of course, been to a European final before when they were washed away by the Brive tide in 1997. But, by 19 May 2001, they had become serial winners: they had already clinched their third successive Premiership title by ending the league season eight points ahead of Wasps, their nearest challengers, and they beat Bath in the new-fangled Zurich Championship final six days before their trip to Paris to play Stade Français in the Heineken Cup final.

It was, by common consent, already the most successful season in Leicester's history but if they were to round it off, they had to beat the French champions in what amounted to their own back yard. Stade Français played then in the little Stade Jean Bouin which lies, literally, in the shadow of the Parc des Princes, the venue for the final, a concrete giant abandoned by the national side when they moved to the Stade de France three years earlier. England players of that era, though, had never minded playing at the Parc; many of them positively welcomed the opportunity.

And Leicester were not short of England players: five of them had played in that year's Six Nations, four more had been capped and Ben Kay and Andy Goode would become internationals. Throw in two more hugely influential figures, Australia's Pat Howard and Ireland's Geordan Murphy, plus Winston Stanley, the Canada wing, and the overall experience was self-evident. What is also

BELOW, BOTH Between them, kickers Tim Stimpson (*right*) and Diego Dominguez scored 49 of the final's 64 total points.

instructive is the players who never won full international honours but were key ingredients on the day: Will Johnson, the younger brother of Martin, the club captain, started in the back row and when he had to be replaced just before half-time, Paul Gustard came on; Jamie Hamilton offered an important cameo at scrum-half, likewise Glen Gelderbloom in the centre. The likes of Lewis Moody, Richard Cockerill and Perry Freshwater were not required off the bench.

Not that Stade Français were short of international experience either. All but Cliff Mytton of their starting XV had been capped, ten by France, two by Canada, one (flanker Richard Pool-Jones) by England and one, Diego Dominguez, by Italy and Argentina. Of those, Dominguez was by far the most dangerous, for his game-management but mainly his point-scoring ability with the boot. The little fly-half did not possess a classical kicking style, he tended to a backward lean more akin to a soccer player's style, but he found the target with monotonous regularity.

In the quarter-finals, Swansea went down in a heap at Leicester and Stade confirmed their position as favourites by disposing of Pau at home. In the last four, Leicester came through 19–15 against Gloucester, requiring more than a hint of

> Neither club made its way to the final unscathed. Leicester had lost 18–11, in pool play, at Pontypridd (six penalty goals by Lee Jarvis for the Welsh club) while Stade Français also lost in Wales, 18–16 to Swansea.

good fortune, while Stade had cause to be grateful there was no video replay available of John O'Neill's disallowed try for Munster, who lost 16–15.

Nervous times indeed; moreover Leicester had been without Martin Johnson for three of their games, injury and suspension forcing England's captain out. As it happened, Johnson also received a yellow card against Gloucester and another in the final, by which time Leicester had learned to manage without one of their

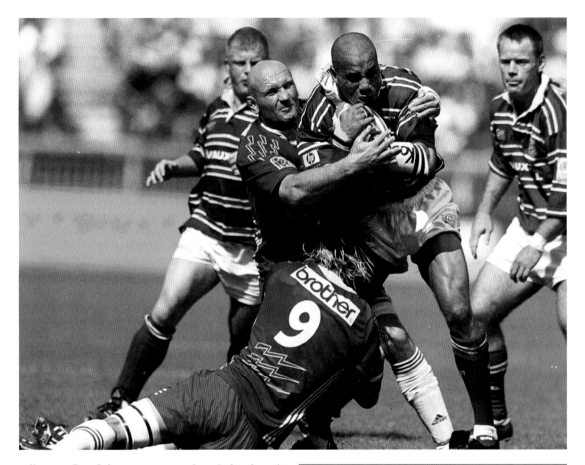

talismen. But Johnson was on the pitch when it mattered, in the closing stages of a tumultuous final played in brilliant sunshine in front of a capacity crowd of 44,300, of whom more than 14,000 travelled from the Midlands.

To rewind that match now is to be amazed at the older Johnson's all-round contribution and for the thought to occur how much the final resembled another match that Johnson played in two years later – the World Cup final against Australia in Sydney. True, for long periods of that second match, England led on the scoreboard while in Paris it was Stade Français who spent most of the match with their noses in front but whereas Elton Flatley's goalkicking constantly pegged England back in 2003, Leicester stayed in this game by scoring tries.

Nor did the Heineken Cup final go to extra time but both matches required a brave and decisive piece of play to discover the winner in the last couple of minutes. In Sydney, Johnson's ice-cold veteran warriors created the opportunity for Jonny Wilkinson's famous dropped goal. In Paris, the architect who clinched victory by 34–30 to the Tigers was Austin Healey, the motormouth, at scrum-half but who was moved to fly-half for the final nine minutes.

The Leicester Lip enjoyed no end the chance to wind others up – he still does, in his role as TV pundit – but there are few with a better understanding of the game, particularly what is required for effective back play. Healey would be the first to acknowledge the contribution of his forward pack as the game unfolded, notably Neil Back whose ability as a flanker both to see space and execute the telling pass was never seen to better effect. But the scrum-half was carrying strained knee ligaments into the game and, at one stage after an accidental collision with Darren Garforth's head, looked unlikely to finish it.

So how fitting that Healey's was the knife that finally sliced Stade Français open. The French club, on reflection, might have seen the match lost during the ten minutes when Johnson was in the sin bin in the third quarter, when their fifteen men went to a 21–14 lead over Leicester's fourteen but only through

Dominguez's penalties of which, during the match, there were a remarkable nine, two of them from well over 50 metres. Stade chose to play a territorial game rather than to stretch Leicester wide and create chances for the lethal Christophe Dominici and the powerful Thomas Lombard.

Leicester had their own booming kicker in Tim Stimpson, whose three penalties had made the half-time score 15–9. A long pass by Back, a cute chip-kick from Howard and Murphy's tap on gave Leon Lloyd the chance to stretch his long legs and score the game's first try immediately after the break. Shortly after Johnson's return, Leicester levelled when Back's dummy fooled the French defence and he nipped over from a close-range ruck, Stimpson's conversion making the score 21–21.

Thereafter it was nip and tuck as the respective kickers duelled, Dominguez throwing in a dropped goal for good measure in the 78th minute to give Stade a 30–27 lead. Leicester's response was immediate. It had to be with the clock running down. Another pass from Back and there was Healey, splitting the defence from forty metres out and then purveying the perfect pass to Lloyd who did not have to break stride and finished, majestically, in the corner. Stimpson's conversion from the touchline meant that not even another goal by Dominguez would suffice; Stade had to score a try with only seconds remaining and throughout the previous eighty minutes they had never threatened to do so.

It was one of those imperfect games that had everything, on a par with the best of internationals, but with that tribalism which became such a feature of the Heineken Cup from the earliest days of European competition. Leicester's post-match celebrations, it is said, were of a similar grand dimension and nearly cost them the cup itself before a saving hand kept the trophy from a home at the bottom of the Seine. As and when that side regroups, twenty, thirty, forty years on, they will think that 2001 was a very special, nay a vintage, year.

It Was Clive Woodward's Woodward's Finest Hour

STEVE BALE

Clive Woodward had more triumphs than the rest of England's coaches put together, probably in quantity as well as most definitely in quality. The 2003 Rugby World Cup victory over which he presided still stands as the acme of the quarter-century professional era and you could argue it exceeded anything from the preceding century and more of amateurism.

But by the time England reached the fateful day against Australia in Sydney they had become a team in decline, and as a performance their final was flawed for all the merits of the grand old-ish men who got them through it, just. It was way short of the thrashing they administered to the Wallabies in Melbourne five months earlier.

No, the greatest of all the performances by Woodward's England came in the much less obvious setting of Vélez Sarsfield, Buenos Aires, when a team reduced mostly to second and even third choices somehow defeated Argentina 26–18. Talk about a triumph in adversity: the Pumas had beaten France, recent Grand Slam winners, 28–27 on the same ground one week earlier.

But it went far deeper than that. Everything about that English visit – two matches, a fortnight in Buenos Aires, so not even a proper tour – was an exercise in prevailing despite, certainly not because of, the English system. If you think there is a continuing debate about player welfare, you're absolutely correct; but it raged just as fiercely leading up to the Atlantic crossing of Phil Vickery's team.

Vickery? 2002? Where to begin with the list of absentees? Martin Johnson was excused after Leicester's second domestic/European double season, though he had missed three weeks of it after one of his periodic run-ins with the Rugby Football Union's disciplinarians. Some other Leicester players were similarly exempt. Vickery was the only one of the 2001 Lions taken to Argentina.

Woodward's first, more obvious idea had been to reappoint Lawrence Dallaglio a couple of years after he had been stripped of the captaincy. Dallaglio had hardly appeared that season after making the Lions tour with a pre-existing knee injury which he duly exacerbated in Australia. 'He won't make the mistake of playing injured like that again,' Woodward had said.

> **BELOW** Lewis Moody, one of the few on the tour who had featured in the Six Nations earlier in the season, is stopped by Diego Albanese. Moody was later selected for RWC2003 and played in the final.

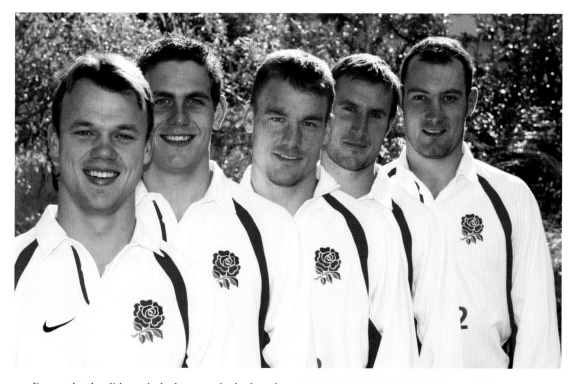

ABOVE (*From left*) new caps Phil Christophers, Ben Johnston, Michael Horak, Geoff Appleford and Alex Codling form a pre-match line-up.

Except that he did precisely that once he had made his club comeback. Having then been restored by Woodward, Dallaglio detached a thumb ligament with Wasps, needing an operation that was postponed to the end of the season while he played on and made it clear his priority was, rather than England, to help his club qualify for the European Cup. In this, at least, he succeeded.

So Vickery it was. He, Steve Thompson, Ben Kay and Lewis Moody were the only first choices from the 2002 Six Nations in the eventual squad. Mishaps abounded: Ed Pearce of Gloucester was married on a Friday, chosen to replace Simon Shaw on the Saturday, had an ankle injury against Bristol at Twickenham later on Saturday and was out of the party almost before he was in it.

By the time they set out Woodward was without 35 players omitted for rest or recuperation, or to make the point a different way, the 30 players who made it had 149 caps – with Joe Worsley and Tim Stimpson with 19 each and Vickery 16 having more than a third of those between them. By comparison, the tour from hell – the 1998 odyssey through Australia, New Zealand and South Africa unfondly remembered as a nadir of English rugby – was deprived of a mere 19 candidates.

It is forgotten these days – well, I had forgotten anyway – that Woodward had the idea of converting Trevor Woodman from a loose-head prop to a hooker. For a while the micro-tour had seemed a possible test-bed for this, perhaps in the non-Test match England played, and lost 29–24, to Argentina A five days before the Test. It never happened. Woodman played prop in that game. And he went on to prop the England scrum, with his Cornish comrade Vickery, at the World Cup final seventeen months later. What's more, it was Vickery, not Woodman, who was taken off by Woodward amid that mayhem to enable Jason Leonard to provide essential stability as André Watson's whistle almost blew England into the Parramatta River.

Woodman was a substitute prop, not hooker, at Vélez Sarsfield but no one was used from the bench. Of that Test XV, Steve Thompson, Vickery and Kay were the only ones to make it to the final XV. Lewis Moody was on the bench in Sydney. Worsley and Andy Gomarsall were also in Australia. As well as Woodman, Mark Regan also made the World Cup squad.

So this was an England team deprived of virtually all its best players, confronting a Pumas team regarded by Woodward himself as the best in the history of Argentinian rugby. Yet England won, and won so well despite a relatively narrow final score that some of the Pumas were arranging the exchange of jerseys five minutes before Alain Rolland blew for no-side.

For Michael Horak and Geoff Appleford, two South Africans with handy Anglo-ancestry, this was their one and only cap. Likewise Alex Codling, who – horror of horrors – played injured. Phil Christophers won two more as a replacement, Ben Johnston another one. Tim Stimpson, for all his nineteen previous Tests, only won one more after Buenos Aires. For Alex Sanderson it was the second of five, the only one as a starter. It was the last of David Flatman's eight caps, his only one starting. Once Woodward was able to reunite his leading men, he no longer had any places for those who had zealously stepped in when they were most needed, in the most unpropitious circumstances.

Rewinding again, contrary to the wishes of every Premiership coach Woodward had badly wanted a tour in the year before England went after the Webb Ellis trophy, and he thought he had one . . . to Fiji, Tonga and Samoa. Which in itself remains surprising, given how England have shied away from the vast inconvenience and discomfort of visiting the islands since they were last in Fiji in 1991.

Funnily enough, that visit had been specific preparation for the '91 World Cup. In 2002, there occurred one of those shambles of which rugby is occasionally guilty. At the very time, late June and early July, when England were due to visit, a World Cup qualifying competition between the three had been arranged. Tonga came last but still qualified, via a repêchage against South Korea. As the England tour had been on the International Board schedule for two years, Twickenham was livid. 'A monumental mess,' groaned RFU chief executive Francis Baron. 'It's important for a World Cup year that we have a serious tour, the stronger the opposition the better,' said Woodward. It worked out at rather less, though in its truncated way it was serious.

If Argentina would not be the boot camp the Pacific might have been, the opposition was probably stronger than any of the island teams, even allowing for the trouble Samoa were to give England in their pool match in Melbourne in 2003. But the plan had been to be away for three weeks – this was Woodward's wish, anyway – and play four fixtures. In the end it came down to two fixtures and two weeks. It was an awfully long way for the pleasure and the Argentina Rugby Union were unimpressed that, having obligingly fitted in England at such short notice, there were very few among them that anyone apart from Felipe Contepomi and Agustin Pichot, Bristol's half-backs at the time, particularly recognised.

But that was how this England victory became Woodward's finest. He was forced to take a disparate gang of players who might otherwise have been no-hopers or never-wozzers, blend them into an international team without notice and then devise a strategy to outsmart and outperform serious opposition who had just beaten

ABOVE Gonzalo Quesada gets a clearance away despite the efforts of Joe Worsley.

BELOW Prop David Flatman makes the initial break prior to setting up Phil Cristophers (*right*) for his successful run to the try-line.

France. In every aspect it was a brilliant personal vindication.

The rugby itself may have fallen short of classic status but England ruffled the Pumas with the strength of their defence, a dry run in its way for defence coach Phil Larder ready for the World Cup, and then by striking with two tries after trailing 12–3 at half-time. Argentina's eventual 18 points were made up entirely of penalties by Gonzalo Quesada.

For the record, Gomarsall's split-second reverse pass put Kay through a narrow gap. Christophers side-stepped away for a second on his debut. Charlie Hodgson converted both and kicked three penalties before Stimpson added a last penalty. 'I had no doubts we could win the game,' Woodward said. 'We should have won by more.' Too true.

This was a curiosity of a momentous occasion, both in its surprising outcome and the negligible effect on many whose Test careers either ended that day or did not go much further. Woodward regarded it as vital proceeding towards the World Cup and it undoubtedly was – perhaps most of all in showing him who of his victorious heroes he could, after all, leave safely behind.

NEXUS

Moving business over the line

As specialist healthcare and education industry advisors and investors we provide a range of business and management services, including:

- Property fund management
- Real estate advisory services
- Education property investment
- Corporate finance advice
- Private equity services
- International Opera Awards
- Investor Publishing: *HealthInvestor UK, HealthInvestor Asia, EducationInvestor Global, NutritionInvestor, Nursery Management Today, Caring Times, Journal of Dementia Care*
- Code Hospitality community

For more information visit:

nexusgroup.co.uk | phpgroup.co.uk
scaleupfund.co.uk | nivl.co.uk
healthinvestor.co.uk | healthinvestorasia.com
educationinvestor.co.uk | nutritioninvestor.com
careinfo.org | nmt-magazine.co.uk
journalofdementiacare.co.uk | thepinefund.com
codehospitality.co.uk | operaawards.org

Property Management

PHP Primary Health Properties

Corporate Finance	Property Investment
NEXUS INVESTMENTS	**NEXUS** PINE

Media

HealthInvestor Asia

NutritionInvestor

Vernon Pugh, The Game Changer

CHRIS THAU

At the beginning of the 1990s the status quo in rugby, sarcastically described as 'Shamateurism', was the main non-playing feature of the game, when Vernon Pugh, QC, a respected barrister and judge, was asked to chair a Welsh Rugby Union inquiry into the involvement of several Welsh players and administrators in the 1989 IRFB-sanctioned rugby tour to South Africa. His report, made available in August 1991, just a few months before the start of the second RWC tournament, mentioned 'an absolutely essential and long overdue ... need for a root and branch reform of both the playing and administrative structure' in Wales. The turmoil that engulfed Welsh rugby following the publication of the report and a subsequent vote of no confidence in the WRU Committee led to the installation of a new committee, which included Pugh, who was then elected WRU Chairman.

It was becoming abundantly clear that defending and policing Corinthian values and principles was now virtually unmanageable as unions, clubs and players had been finding ways to bypass the rules and regulations. In an attempt to stem the tide, the amateur regulations were reviewed at an IRFB meeting in October 1993, and again at the IRFB General Assembly in Vancouver in 1994, but neither the unions nor the players and clubs played ball, so the abuse went on. It was clear that the amateur regulations were no longer fit for purpose. In 1994, Vernon Pugh became the elected chair of an IRFB Amateurism Working Party, alongside Bernard Lapasset of France, Rob Fisher of New Zealand and Fred McLeod of Scotland. In March 1995, their paper on amateurism was circulated among the member unions, though, as Pugh himself acknowledged, the board was not ready to consider a 'pay for play' option.

A few months later, during the third RWC tournament in 1995, an astounding US$550 million TV deal was announced between the emerging force of international sports broadcasting, Sky Sports, and the three leading Southern Hemisphere unions. This changed radically the parameters of the game, providing the three unions with the financial clout that enabled them to fight off a far more daring and ambitious pirate project, the bid of the World Rugby Corporation (WRC) in effect to buy the top players around the world and take control of the game. The WRC's brazen attempt to take over the world of rugby concentrated the minds of the game's leading administrators, one of whom was Vernon Pugh, by now appointed, through rotation, Chairman of the IRFB. In this capacity Pugh launched a massive campaign to restore the dented status of the game's governing body and to make all union administrators, players and officials, and the potential commercial partners, aware of the need to accept and respect the laws of the game and the IRFB regulations. 'The rules have to be complied with. There is no option for any country or club to proceed independently,' he was quoted as saying on any number of occasions.

LEFT Vernon Pugh at an IRB press conference in 1999.

RIGHT HM the Queen, Keith Rowlands, chief executive of RWC1999, and Vernon Pugh, with the Webb Ellis trophy during the 1999 tournament.

BELOW Vernon Pugh celebrates with the winning New Zealand players after they clinched the 2000–2001 World Sevens Series.

In the meantime, the three Southern Hemisphere unions, engaged in a brutal clash with the agents of the WRC, used the funds from Sky TV to weather the storm by offering their leading players better financial packages to tempt them to reject the WRC offers. They succeeded. As SARFU Chairman Louis Luyt acknowledged at the Paris meeting, 'Whilst News Corporation only bought the TV rights of the Southern Hemisphere, WRC bought all the rights and the players body and soul . . . I can say that the players now belong to SARFU. Because what we've done, we've taken the WRC contract, substituted WRC for SARFU, and that's exactly where we stand.' And that was true for New Zealand and Australia as well, though the NZRU council had already voted to repeal the amateur regulations in December 1994.

> **ABOVE** The four members of the IRFB Amateurism Working Party: (left to right) Rob Fisher (New Zealand), Bernard Lapasset (France), Vernon Pugh (Wales, chairman), Fred McLeod (Scotland).
> **BELOW RIGHT** Toulouse and Munster pause for a minute's silence before the Heineken Cup semi-final, 26 April 2003, in memory of IRB Chairman Vernon Pugh who had died two days previously.

Meanwhile Pugh had been preparing for the biggest and final battle of the amateur era, a Special Meeting of the IRFB Council in Paris at the end of August 1995. At the meeting, the succinct and forensically accurate Amateurism Working Party Report was adopted without a murmur of dissent. The acceptance without disagreement of a report that concluded that the game had basically crossed the threshold and could not describe itself any more as bona fide amateur, made a vote unnecessary and paved the way for perhaps the greatest morning in the history of Rugby Football. Had someone challenged the findings of the report, or even questioned it, the outcome of the day might have been different.

In a stroke of genius, Pugh identified that the dispute was no longer between amateur and professional; but between retaining control of the game and losing it to commercial forces and made this the centrepiece of his argument revealed with prudence and great intellectual rigour. After welcoming the gathered officials in Welsh with a warm '*Bore-da pawb*', he underlined the historic significance of the occasion: 'We have a formidable task ahead of us and it is essentially to decide the future of the game as something, which can be seen as lasting, practical, and introduce us into what is certainly a new era for rugby union football,' he said in a messianic mode. And that set the tone of the most amazing day of revelations and confessions, in the history of rugby football, as the three major Southern Hemisphere unions, as well as the majority of the delegates acknowledged that in their jurisdictions, the game had gone professional, in all but name.

It started with Rob Fisher of New Zealand, who explained that to all intents and purposes New Zealand had already decided to go professional almost a year before, and that virtually all All Black players had signed professional contracts with the NZRU. He was followed by South Africa's Louis Luyt, who confirmed that the Springboks were now paid to play 'We are professional' he said, and Australia's Roger Vanderfield, who by and large mirrored the New Zealand case. By the end of the morning everyone had more or less confessed, with the exception of Argentina's Carlos Tozzi and Canada's Alan Sharp, who had no case to answer, while both Italy's Maurizio Mondelli and Shiggy Kono of Japan explained that the two unions were unable to control the excesses of their clubs. England and France had agreed that the current situation was untenable, likewise the Scots and the Welsh, while in Ireland, as Syd Millar acknowledged, the players were hedging their bets waiting to see the outcome of the debate. The following morning at the press conference Pugh spelt out the unanimous decision: 'Subsequent to the repeal of the amateur regulations, rugby will become an open game. There will be no prohibition on payment or the provision of any other material benefit to any person involved in the game.'

The audacious decision to abandon a century of amateur tradition, though widely praised, remained controversial for mainly sentimental reasons and triggered off a series of unforeseen events, made worse by some misguided administrative decisions and/or inaction by the RFU and WRU in particular. To start with, several investors took the opportunity to purchase at very ill-defined prices whole clubs on both sides of the Anglo-Welsh border, which complicated matters further. The New Zealand model of centralised contracts for the elite players was rebuffed, mostly from ignorance, or obduracy, which gave the club owners in England and Wales a chance to take over control of the players and start to dictate terms to the toothless unions.

The RFU produced a meaningless 'Right to Decide' paper that delayed any action for a whole year, while the Welsh Union was engulfed in a bitter 'civil war' with a number of clubs who tried to break away. To make matters worse, in June 1996 the RFU sold the TV rights to England Five Nations home matches, previously shared with the other nations, to Sky Sports for £87.5 million for five years. In July, led by Vernon Pugh, the remaining four unions, which significantly included France, voted to exclude England from the Five Nations, a major step that forced Twickenham to reconsider its break-away move. By September 1996 the rebellion had been quelled and the Five Unions signed the famous 'Accord' that has remained the main guideline for their relations to this day. By this time the club owners had been openly challenging the right of the unions to run the game in their territory and again the tenacity and foresight of Vernon Pugh and his group of like-minded administrators in Ireland, Scotland and France helped to save the day.

The premature death of Vernon Pugh QC, on 24 April 2003, at the age of fifty-seven, deprived the game of an inspiring figure at a time when his leadership and vision were most needed. He passed away a couple of days before the final RWC2003 qualifier, the repêchage match between the USA and Spain in Fort Lauderdale, Florida, which saw the US Eagles capture the twentieth and final slot in the 2003 tournament line-up.

EASTDIL SECURED

is proud to support

Wooden Spoon Rugby World

EASTDIL SECURED

The Real Estate Investment Banking Company

London | Dubai | Dublin | Frankfurt | Hong Kong | Paris | Tokyo

New York | Los Angeles | Atlanta | Boston | Chicago | Charlotte | Dallas | Seattle | Silicon Valley | Orange County | Washington D.C.

www.eastdilsecured.com

Dad's Army Win the World Cup

SIR CLIVE WOODWARD

I t can be a bit strange looking back on Rugby World Cup 2003 and everything that went with England's success that year. Sometimes it feels like ancient history, another lifetime, consisting of cherished memories and anecdotes that are firmly in a corner of my mind to be accessed whenever I am asked. But on other occasions, for no good reason I can think of, I am suddenly right there again living it in real time, mulling over an important selection or working out what our order of penalty takers would be if we were still level with Australia after extra time in the final! What fun that would have been by the way.

It was such a busy vivid time and many memories – often very personal ones – seared themselves into my mind without me really registering them at the time and they only come out years later when there is the leisure to process them.

It hadn't been a straightforward time for me or England after I was appointed coach in 1997, the first professional coach of the national team lest we forget. For a start there was the whole novelty of how does this work exactly? There was no manual, no set protocols on how much access the England coach had to professional club players. It was very much trial and error. And there were no facilities. Famously the first thing I had to do was ask Don Rutherford, the RFU Technical Director, for an office, a phone and a computer.

There were some bumps on the road, or learning experiences as some coaches euphemistically call painful defeats, although I am of the strong opinion that you actually learn most from your best wins and victories. They were the games I always analysed and got all the squad to review and commit to their minds and muscle memory. I mostly tended to 'bin' the frustrating defeats and poor performances. Accentuate the positive, eliminate the negative

The Tour from Hell in 1998 – planned long before my time – could have derailed us before we had even started the journey and was pretty painful at the time but ultimately it served a useful purpose and I identified a few younger players – Matt Dawson, Phil

> **PREVIOUS PAGE** Sir Clive after RWC2003, with the Webb Ellis trophy.
>
> **BELOW**: Martin Johnson sets up another England drive in the World Cup final, with Mike Tindall in support.

Vickery, Jonny Wilkinson, Josh Lewsey and Lewis Moody in particular – who were made of the right stuff going forward.

ABOVE England's Ben Kay loses possession almost on the tryline in the tackle of Australia's Phil Waugh.

Then we blew three Grand Slams in a row in the final games in 1999, 2000 and 2001. The first two were down to our naivety and, frankly, not yet being good enough to close out big 'must-win' matches. I will always maintain, however, that we got unlucky in 2001 when the foot and mouth epidemic intervened just when we were playing our most expansive ever rugby. We were on fire in those first four games. Six months later, when we completed the tournament with a defeat in Ireland, most of the guys were out on their feet after a Lions summer tour, we had lost all momentum and hadn't been able to arrange a warm-up match while the Irish had already played Scotland and Wales. Circumstances contrived against us in 2001 but I remained confident. In fact we didn't look back after that disappointment at Lansdowne Road.

All those hard yards were in our legs, including an ultimately unsuccessful RWC1999 campaign, as we approached 2003 and suddenly everything clicked. A coach dreams of this happening – that fabled lightbulb moment when everything makes sense and your team takes flight – but it rarely does. Suddenly England emerged as world-beaters in front of my very eyes. And when that happens it's pretty much a case of riding the wave, not doing anything to change the magic.

We beat all the SANZAR countries at Twickenham in the autumn of 2002 and absolutely

> Of course our World Cup triumph started well before we got to Australia, well before 2003 in fact, even if that was when everything we had worked for came gloriously together.

roared into 2003. We were incredibly fit, playing at a fiendish tempo that most struggled to live with, and had added a little hard-earned pragmatism to our game. We looked untouchable in the Six Nations and you could argue our greatest-ever performance was going to Dublin again in a Grand Slam decider and on this occasion clinching it with an almost faultless 42–6 win over a really strong Ireland side who were also going for the Slam.

I wasn't worried about peaking too early in 2003; we were on a mission, everybody had bought into the work ethic and sacrifices required. I wanted England to travel to the World Cup as the world number one-ranked

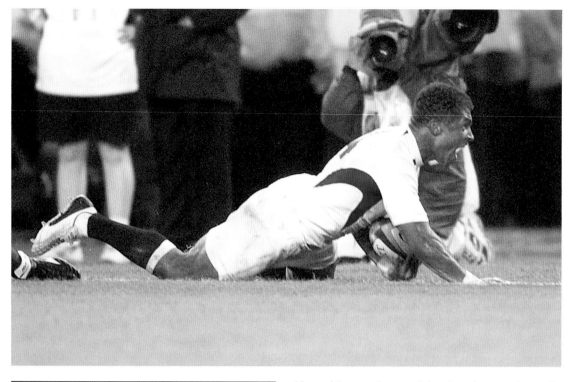

side and I wanted us to claim victories over Australia and New Zealand on a short summer tour we were committed to. Everybody told me it was a tour too far or that I should take a B team and rest my A XV but I – and the team – wanted those scalps on the road. We travelled down south and it was the perfect classic smash and grab tour with wins over New Zealand, New Zealand Maori and Australia.

We would return to Australia three months later with no psychological hang-ups. Just for once the others could worry about us and as soon as the Aussie media started to label us as 'Dad's Army' I knew they were worried all right.

I've spoken about the pure rugby memories concerning 2003 many times so I won't dwell on them too much – you've probably read many of them before – but I will briefly mention a few that most readily come to mind, a top five if you like.

There was the team refusing to do any sort of lap of honour after a terrific semi-final win over France, in fact they scarcely acknowledged the England supporters as Martin Johnson led them back down the tunnel. The team had won nothing yet and they knew it and they wanted the fans to appreciate that as well. Remember those three Slams that slipped from our grasp. Mentally they were in a great place.

Then there was the precision and execution of Jason Robinson's try in the final while another memorable moment was 40,000 English voices singing 'Swing Low' when Jonny went down with what looked a very bad knock as they almost willed him back to full fitness. Remembering moments like that still makes the hairs on the back of my neck stand up.

With my coach's hat on, the team executing the pre-called and much rehearsed zigzag move to set up Jonny for the match-winning dropped goal was magical, and for sheer relief it was Trevor Woodman – a natural footballer not just a fine prop – reacting to Australia's quick restart after Jonny's dropped goal and taking the kick-off perfectly before laying it back. Job done.

As I am sitting writing here today, however, it is the more personal memories that keep forcing their way into my mind. When we finally got back to the dressing room and when the last VIP guest had left – Princes Harry and William had looked in along with the late Tessa Jowell who was Minister of Sport and had supported me so much – all of my coaching team headed for the coaches' changing room. There were benches and chairs but for some reason to a man we just sat on the floor with our backs against the walls. There were just seven of us, myself, Andy Robinson, Phil Larder, Dave Alred, Simon Hardy, Phil Keith-Roache and Dave Reddin. We sat, beers in hand, in complete and utter silence for what seemed an eternity just taking in what had just

ABOVE Jonny Wilkinson kicked four penalties in addition to the winning drop-goal.

RIGHT Australia's George Gregan is bundled into touch by Ben Kay as assistant referee Paddy O'Brien looks on.

happened. Then Phil Larder piped up. 'Well what the xxxx are we going to do now?' It was just a magic moment with a brilliant group of people who I will never forget and a very good question as it turned out!

About 2.30 a.m. a few of us decided it was time to head back to the hotel from the official function down at the harbour. There was just Jayne and me, and Jonny and his then girlfriend Dai Stewart in the minibus; the rest had gone into Sydney. It was a lovely quiet drive at that time of night and actually a drive I had done hundreds of times before when I lived in Manly. And then, about 3.00 a.m., we pulled around the corner and there was our hotel, the Manly Pacific, totally besieged

ABOVE England's Will Greenwood (*left*) celebrates with match-winning hero Jonny Wilkinson on the final whistle.

by thousands of England supporters. We were the first of the England party back and when Jonny stepped out the place went totally bonkers – his life especially was never going to be the same again.

The graciousness of Eddie Jones and his Australian team in defeat was something I had not seen before from him and this stays with me. Myself and Eddie had been enjoying our normal banter in the build-up but for some reason I went straight to him on the final whistle. No words were needed – it could have been a bit awkward as we were hardly the best of friends then – we shook hands, he said 'Well done mate, congratulations. Now get off and celebrate with your team, we're OK.' Deep down he knew the better team had won but he was hurting. George Gregan and all the Aussie team couldn't have been more complementary afterwards either. The entire Aussie team were class in defeat.

Talking of class, I must mention the contribution of those who did not make the match-day 22 as it was in those days. I announced the team on the Tuesday morning to the squad and it was not a difficult selection but at no time did those not picked allow their personal disappointment to show or affect the team's preparation. Make no mistake if one player goes walkabout it can cost you the World Cup final. I can name these players just as easily as I can the starting XV: Julian White, Mark Regan, Simon Shaw, Joe Worsley, Andy Gomarsall, Paul Grayson, Dan Luger and Stuart Abbot. They all played a vital role which will not be forgotten by anybody in the squad.

That I should be living out these extraordinary times in Manly – England were based in Manly – was quite surreal. Jayne and I had lived there for five years in the late eighties when I played for and captained Manly; we got married there and our first two children, Jess and Joe, were born there; it will always be a very special place. The deal with the kids in 2003 was simple – if we made the final we would fly both Jess and Joe out. So as soon as we beat France in the semi-final Jayne spent a day on the phone arranging for them to fly out for four days to take the final in; our other son Freddie was too young to make the trip and is still cranky that he didn't make the cut.

We were living the dream and the culmination of that dream was the parade around London soon after we got back. The number of fans in Sydney at the final and phone calls and messages from back home had given us some idea of the reaction but frankly nothing had really prepared us for the full force of the public's response. Our parade and celebrations in Trafalgar Square were amazing memories. Our success in 2003 changed the lives of all those concerned, both the achievement there and then and the future opportunities it threw up for many of those involved. It was a golden time

Wales Grand Slam – Lions Well Beaten

DAVID STEWART

Walking past Cardiff Castle shortly after dawn on the Sunday morning, a glance down St Mary Street – home to many of the 'after dark' venues – revealed a scene resembling the last days of Rome, as the Council Cleansing team started their onerous task. Tarmacadam was barely visible through the general detritus, plus an occasional human form. Self-evidently, it had been quite some party.

A day earlier, Wales had won their first Grand Slam since 1979; the first Triple Crown since 1988; and first Championship since 1994, the Alan Davies era. As full time approached in the Millennium Stadium, and home support reached a classic crescendo, in the commentary box Brian Moore said perceptively: 'I get it now; for the first time I really understand what this means to the Welsh.'

It was a memorable few days. By morning coffee on Saturday 19 March, thousands were already sitting by a big screen on the area of green between Cardiff's Civic Centre and the Hilton. The sun was cracking the stones. Even on St Patrick's weekend, one had a notion it wasn't going to be the visitors' day – perhaps the Irish squad, resident in said hotel, picked up the same vibe.

From the moment Gethin Jenkins charged down a Ronan O'Gara clearing kick fifteen minutes in, matters unfolded accordingly. The 'afters' continued through Sunday. A splendid *Rugby Special* (of fond memory) was hosted by John Inverdale in the Cardiff RFC clubhouse, with Mike Ruddock – the epitome of decency – as primary guest. Naturally, filming took place in the middle of another 'session'. Eventually celebrations were wrapped up at the Butchers Arms in Llandaff, some time on the Monday evening.

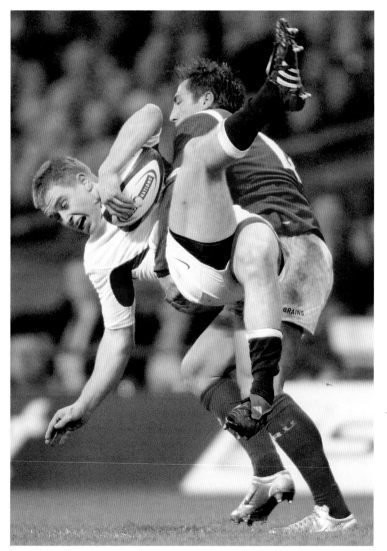

It all started seven weeks earlier. The English came to Cardiff on the Championship's opening day. Andy Robinson, head coach for the first time in a Six Nations contest, raised eyebrows on both sides of the Severn Bridge by including the hugely promising Matthew Tait – a day short of his nineteenth birthday – in the key berth of outside centre. An early intervention by Gavin Henson saw the young Newcastle player comprehensively dumped on his backside. The tone was set.

8–9 down, deep into the last ten minutes, a penalty on half-way was awarded to the home side. Outside the range of Stephen Jones, up stepped the Bridgend

LEFT Setting down a marker for the tournament: Gavin Henson welcomes Matthew Tait to international rugby.

ABOVE RIGHT Shane Williams sets up to sidestep past Ireland fly-half Ronan O'Gara.

lad (hitherto best known to many for his fake tan and carefully prepared hair) and booted it over. 'Shave away, Gavin, shave away,' said Eddie Butler on the BBC, in reference to the smoothly groomed thighs of the inside centre.

Wales were on their way. Rome was next, where two years earlier they had stumbled badly – Colin Charvis, skipper, caught on camera smiling at an unfortunate moment, as they slid to defeat. No problem this time: a comfortable 8–38.

On the middle weekend, a trickier assignment awaited in Paris. The French were bested 18–24, but not before a nine-point deficit at the interval was overcome, without Gareth Thomas – the captain departed the tournament exactly mid-way through, due to a wrist injury. The old firm of Williams and Jones did the scoring: Martyn with two tries, Stephen a full house of penalties, conversions and a drop.

In the final away game, Scotland – a bit of a mess, coach Matt Williams having 'lost the dressing room' – were being trounced 3–43 early in the second half, before restoring some respectability by pulling back to 22–46 at no-side. Try scorers this time included Shane and Rhys (Williams) and Ryan (Jones).

Ireland represented the last hurdle. Two Pontypridd men stepped forward. Michael Owen, a calm and intelligent presence at the back of the scrum, had taken over the leadership baton; his ensemble didn't miss a beat. Kevin Morgan, diminutive and injury-prone, had his finest moments in the international game – a delightful footballer, he had moved from 14 to 15 when Thomas was crocked, scoring three tries in the final two games.

An official match report described the finale as 'a scrappy, error-ridden contest'. Not a soul in Wales will have cared; that party could begin.

A continuum of sorts flowed from that wonderful early spring Saturday. Understandably, plenty of Welshmen were selected for the Lions tour. Clive Woodward's insistence on a mega-large squad – and a budget to match

– necessitated a fund-raising warm-up game before heading to New Zealand, So, the Argentinians came to Cardiff. In a portent of things to come down south, a largely second-string Pumas line-up held the Lions XV to a 25–25 draw.

Some 2005 Lions spoke well of the management skills displayed by Sir Clive on that trip. Others did not, and the record book is harsh: Test defeats by margins of 21–3, 48–18 and 38–19.

Woodward's primary defence, when reviewing the series, was that New Zealand were particularly strong. True, but the core of the team for the First Test had not played together, line-out calls were changed that week (this under a man who set great store on attention to detail), and his selection relied too heavily on veterans from Sydney 2003 (Robinson, Wilkinson, Back, Hill, Kay).

Neither Ryan Jones (by general consensus, the player of the tour) nor Simon Easterby were among eight back-row forwards originally chosen, yet both started in the back row for the last two Tests.

There is mitigation. A suspicion lingers that Lawrence Dallaglio, while not captain, was intended to be the heartbeat of the squad. His loss, early in the tour opener against Bay of Plenty, was a heavy blow. Then, in arctic-like Christchurch, tour captain Brian O'Driscoll was cruelly taken out in the opening match of the series. When it comes to culpability, New Zealanders – players, media and supporters – have been disappointingly mealy-mouthed ever since.

No fewer than eleven changes – some injury-enforced, and including positional shifts – were made by the time the Lions' leviathan arrived in Wellington. The 'Cake Tin' Test went down as Carter's match – Dan's finest hour. The series gone, a third defeat in Auckland had an air of *fin de siècle*. A whitewash, as in 1966 and 1983, was the predictable outcome.

On his return to England, Woodward pursued a brief flirtation with Southampton FC, and has not subsequently re-entered serious rugby coaching. The intervening years have allowed participants to record their own conclusions.

Brian O'Driscoll: 'I describe it as deliberate foul play, dangerous, a cheap shot.'

Paul O'Connell: 'We came across an excellent side, and we never became the team we needed to be.'

Shane Williams: 'We had no answer for what they threw at us, and that was not only a shedload of skill and physicality, but a pride I had never previously encountered. There was no way they were going to allow a British & Irish Lions team to come to their territory and win.'

As the years passed, so Woodward himself became philosophical: 'With hindsight, I was probably the wrong choice.* When that first Test came, I should have gone with form; instead I went with the players I knew had never let me down.'

Ian McGeechan was an assistant coach on the tour, heading up the 'Midweek Massive' (as the T & Ws styled themselves). In his autobiography, the most travelled Lion of all was typically forensic, if cloaked in characteristic politeness:

'There were fifty-one Lions who played on tour and two enormous management teams. In theory it sounded good but it missed the boat by being far too cumbersome for a five-week build-up to the Tests.

'Paul O'Connell, who four years later was my captain for the 2009 tour to South Africa, has said that the players never really got to know each other properly because they were always going their separate ways. He also remarked that they were never sure who was who, and who did what, among the management team.

'Some Lions hardly saw each other and others hardly played. The outcome was disastrous – a kind of Test series we had never seen before. It was bitterly disappointing. The All Blacks were *not as good as we made them look* [writer's italics].

'Clive became a little too anxious, concerned perhaps that New Zealand had inside information, or at least were desperately trying to pick up secrets from our camp. He convinced himself the All Blacks had tapped into our line-out signals, so we changed them all the week before the First Test. At half-time players were still asking themselves where they had to stand for certain calls.'

Let us leave the final words to Chris Hewett, writing in this august publication fifteen years ago: 'the biggest squad, the most lavish support – medical, logistical, technical, financial, you name it – and, sadly, the greatest rugby disappointment of our age'.

* A personal beef is that, with the exception of Sir Clive, we have to go back to 1983 and Jim Telfer (leaving aside Mick Doyle, appointed for the cancelled 1986 South Africa trip) to find someone other than Sir Ian McGeechan or a New Zealander who has been Lions head coach. Readers may think that is a rather depressing record, when there are four home countries to choose from.

BELOW Lewis Moody probably wishes he had chosen a different route off the field after the Lions' overwhelming 48–18 loss in the Second Test.

Northern Lights Shine at Sale

STEPHEN JONES

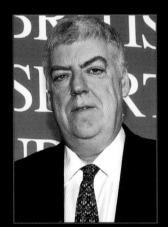

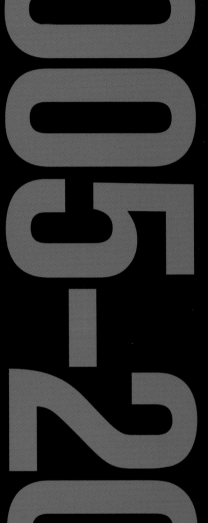
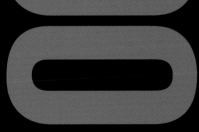

2005–2006

The domestic season of 2005/6 began in British and Irish rugby under the darkest of clouds. The Lions had just endured the most torturous tour of New Zealand when, under Sir Clive Woodward, they had been thrashed by 3–0 in the Test series by the All Blacks, in what became a humiliation long before the end. Woodward was later to admit that he had things all wrong and so, when his dishevelled party arrived home, we all looked for evidence in the domestic season that we Brits could still play the game.

As ever, the season was packed, not always with epic rugby. But as it progressed, those who keenly desired some new faces had their wishes granted. Sale Sharks had been one of the better teams in England for a long time; even when they were still at their homely Heywood Road, they were successful, reaching the Pilkington Cup Final in 1998. Fashionable they probably were not, but momentum was growing.

> Saint-André realised that the success in the English game usually lay up front, and he began to establish a formidable pack of forwards in which the signature player was a giant prop, Andrew Sheridan.

In 2004, they took a gamble by appointing as director of rugby the French wing, Philippe Saint-André, who had won 69 caps for his country, played throughout the momentous 1995 World Cup and also played and coached at Gloucester. He had been the man who started the 'Try from the End of the World', that fantastic effort scored by the 1994 French touring team in New Zealand at Christchurch, which sealed a staggering 2–0 series victory over the All Blacks.

When he arrived at Sale it was after some controversies. Although he is much revered at Gloucester his tenure there did not end well, and even though he was then linked with several other coaching jobs nothing came to fruition until Brian Kennedy, then the owner of Sale, signed him to act in what was intended to be an overall role, in charge of the team and also of trying to lay down a platform for a successful future.

Le Goret ('the piglet', because of his shuffling style of running) duly took the reins and season 2004/5 saw Sale growing further in stature.

At the start of season 2005/6 the progress continued. At that stage Sale – they had had to move out of the tiny Heywood Road – were playing their home games at Edgeley Park, the home of Stockport County. No one could pretend that it was a glamorous location: it was difficult to get to on a Friday evening – when Sale played most of their games – and even though it was an efficient kind of stadium it was on a confined site, and of course shared with a football team.

But it had something. There was a cavernous covered standing area at one end, originally intended for the home football fans but which was gradually adopted by the Sale followers and they turned it into a party arena for those Friday home games. It became the spot in which to shout and to be seen, and when Sale were hammering away trying to score at that end it became electric.

And Saint-André & Co. were building extremely well. Sale were rapidly off the mark in what turned out to be a fantastic season.

RIGHT: Charlie Hodgson kicks at goal during the Premiership final. Hodgson scored six penalties and a drop goal.

They had several trademarks but one of them was an ability to get the ball away into midfield in what seemed to be a matter of three or four seconds. Chris Jones, the lanky line-out jumper, was light and could be lifted to the stars by his props and often Sale would take the ball off the top of his jump, the emerging Richard Wigglesworth would ship the ball to Charlie Hodgson in midfield and Sale would be over the gain line before anyone had blinked.

But there were other key men in that team. The trademark player was unquestionably the volcanic Sebastien Chabal, the bearded French number 8. When he was on the rampage carrying the ball, there was no more arresting sight in the whole of rugby. People claimed that he was often lax in defence, and that his game did have weaknesses – and it is fair to say that he was not always trusted by the French selectors. But he was to be the signature player of the 2007 World Cup, dominating the country on giant poster sites, portrayed as 'The Caveman'.

It was he who dragged Sale onto the front foot so often and he was also part of one of the best back rows to have appeared in the Premiership. Sale had Magnus Lund on the open side, still one of the heroes of the club's existence. And on the blind side was Jason White, who had moved down from Scotland and soon reached world class playing for club and country.

Saint-André had bought in two imports to boost the pack in Lionel Faure from France and Ignacio Fernández Lobbe, the Argentina lock. In the backs, together with the brilliant Jason Robinson and Mark Cueto, Sale could field the Welsh international centre Mark Taylor, the Samoan Elvis Seveali'i and the Spaniard, Oriel Ripol. Throughout the squad there was a sound basis of the north-west's finest to go with the exciting foreign imports.

Sale, sensationally, dominated the Premiership, they finished on 74 points, a full six points ahead of Leicester at the top of the table with London Irish third and Wasps fourth and both Sale and Leicester came through to the Twickenham final which provided the climax to the season. Sale's crowds had averaged in five figures, establishing them in the professional era

Even though Sale had been the better team down the stretch of the Premiership's regular season, they were significant outsiders in the betting against a Leicester team that was used to success and whose players were used to Twickenham, both for their club and their country. Sale also went in without the massive Sheridan, who was injured.

What followed was a sensation at the time and still rings down the ages. Sale gave a brilliant performance to win 45–20, dominating large areas of the match. The immaculate Hodgson kicked six penalties, but Sale also scored four tries – from Cueto, Lund, Ripol and their flourishing signature write-off was a try run in from near their own line, with replacement back Chris Mayor racing away triumphantly.

This all constituted an earthquake for the sport, it meant that Sale had joined the hierarchy in the club game, and they have largely remained as contenders near the top ever since, despite the fact that they lack a good deal in natural resources when compared to the great town and city clubs further to the south. For Leicester it was a numbing result. The Sale team subsided a little in the subsequent season, chiefly because they suffered a horrendous run of injury, but they had put themselves on the map, and students of the English game would always recall the Sale charge as one of the real dramas of the whole season.

Saint-André's career continued to be a switchback. He seemed the perfect choice to coach the French national team but when he did so, with the country disunited and clubs and the national union always at war, he simply could not establish himself and lost the job after a cringing 62–13 defeat at the hands of New Zealand.

But in Sale, even to this day, *Le Goret* is revered. Bizarrely, the eclectic team of the Premiership chosen by a distinguished panel that year named only one Sale player – Lund. But just for once, and yet hopefully not for the last time, the epicentre of English rugby had moved north of Watford, north-west of Birmingham, and to the suburbs of Manchester. It was all unique, and so welcome.

Yet there were other dramatic events across rugby. The year 2006 saw Munster finally fulfil their dream of winning the Heineken Cup. They beat Biarritz by 23–19 in a final at the Millennium Stadium which was not as close as the final score suggests – Biarritz at the time were a renowned cup-fighting team but they were bitterly disappointing in the big one and now that they languish in Pro D2 in France, it seems that they may never win a major title. The celebrations after the final almost rivalled those after Welsh rugby internationals and the Munster men were to take the crown again in 2008.

In fact, Declan Kidney's team had an inauspicious start to the campaign, losing away at Sale in the opening round of pool matches but, led by Anthony Foley, who was so sadly to pass away with a heart attack in 2016, they won all their remaining games and went through as pool winners. In the knock-out stages they beat Perpignan 19–10 at fortress Thomond Park – at that stage they had never lost a home Heineken Cup match. Then, in front of a capacity crowd at Lansdowne Road, Foley's men demolished their neighbours Leinster by 30–6 with Ronan O'Gara scoring twenty points.

Yet in 2005–6, defence in rugby was still over-shadowing attack. In the Six Nations, France lost at

> **BELOW**: The Sale Squad celebrate with the trophy following their convincing 45–20 victory.

Murrayfield on the opening weekend but won the Six Nations for the third time in five seasons under the coaching of Bernard Laporte. But any hopes that this made them powerful contenders for the World Cup which France hosted in 2007, were to be brutally dashed.

Ireland celebrated their second Triple Crown in three seasons in the 2006 Championship, Scotland achieved their best-ever Six Nations finish – at the end they stood third; England were fourth. And Italy managed an away draw in Cardiff, 18–18, which still remains one of the best results in their history in the Six Nations. But nothing that year was vintage in the biggest annual tournament of them all.

So in the end, the Lions tour was overtaken by other thrilling events; Sale and Munster were able to lord it over the more familiar Cup winners. There was never really the sense that British and Irish rugby as a whole was lifting itself for an assault on the decades-long authority of the Southern Hemisphere – but the delightful barking of the Northern underdog enlivened the whole season.

LEFT Scrum-half Dimitri Yachvili gets his pass away during the Heineken final. Yachvili kicked 14 of his team's 19 points.

BELOW Munster locks Paul O'Connell (*left*) and Donncha O'Callaghan with the Heineken trophy.

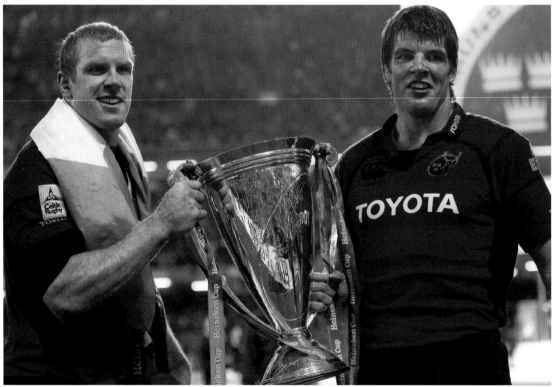

'They'll Never Try That Again'

NEALE HARVEY

I n the immortal words of a pal of mine, 'They'll never try that again.' He had turned to me as the London Wasps players assembled for a second close-range line-out in the thirty-fourth minute of a thrilling first all-English Heineken Cup final against the recently crowned Premiership champions, Leicester.

The 'that' in question was a beautifully crafted front of the line-out routine that had undone Leicester earlier in the half. Wasps' No. 9 Eoin Reddan had sneaked into a space vacated by Leicester's dozing forwards, taken a short throw from hooker Raphael Ibanez and dotted down before anybody could blink. The notion that Tigers might fall for such a ploy again was laughable.

Wasps were leading 8–6 in front of a record crowd of 81,076 for a European final. Leicester had come into the game fully loaded on the back of their 44–16 Premiership Final thrashing of Gloucester and, having also clinched the EDF Energy Anglo-Welsh Cup against the Ospreys a month earlier, a side boasting

It remains one of those 'I was there' moments and you just knew that Leicester would fail in their attempt to become the first English side to secure a domestic and European 'treble'. Despite the presence on the Londoners' coaching staff of giants of the game such as Sir Ian McGeechan, Shaun Edwards and Craig Dowd, it was a little-known Kiwi, Leon Holden, who would later be credited with exposing a fatal flaw in Leicester's defensive armoury.

TOP Raphael Ibanez celebrates Wasps' second cheeky try from a well-worked line-out routine.

immense England World Cup-winning forwards Ben Kay, Lewis Moody, Martin Corry and Julian White was surely not going to be outsmarted in an area of expertise again.

Seconds later, the scoreline read 13–6, leaving 40,000 Wasps fans jubilant and Leicester's hefty travelling contingent rubbing their eyes in disbelief as another lightning strike at the front of the set-piece – this time a quick-fire one-two between Ibanez and Simon Shaw – gave the former space to belt over for a brilliant try that left Tigers' bevy of Test stars in a state of stunned disbelief.

RIGHT Wasps playmaker Alex King gets a clearance kick away.

BELOW Leicester Tigers captain Martin Corry has a brief dispute with Phil Vickery of Wasps.

Sir Ian recalls: 'We knew Leicester put Julian White at the front of the line-out in a defensive role and then he'd go into the line-out to do any support work. Leon Holden identified it and we talked through three options we could use to attack that space. What chuffed us most as coaches was that they were all slightly different set-ups and Leicester couldn't pick up the fact we'd do it again.

'It was cleverly worked out by Leon, but then doing it in practice was even more satisfying. We actually executed our third move at the start of the second half when we got James Haskell around the front of the line-out, but unfortunately there was a forward pass, otherwise we'd have been in for that one again. But to score two tries that won us the match off it was very pleasing.'

While Leicester at that time were the epitome of professionalism under their Aussie director of rugby Pat Howard and were unaccustomed to being outsmarted, in McGeechan, Edwards and their vastly experienced hooker, Ibanez, they met their match.

Another major and successful coaching move prior to the contest had been the inclusion of academy loosehead Tom French in the Wasps starting XV. Former Harrow schoolboy French, 23, had been on loan at National League outfit Henley all season and had never started a game for Wasps, let alone one of such magnitude. And yet, with regular loosehead Tim Payne out injured, French was thrown in and played a blinder, much to the chagrin of Leicester's volatile forwards coach, Richard Cockerill – as McGeechan now reveals.

'We had a three-week gap between our last league game and that Heineken Cup final and at the end of the second week we played a full-on practice match between ourselves at our training ground in Acton,' McGeechan explained. 'We spoke to Raphael Ibanez about the front row and we thought the thing to do was to put Phil Vickery at No. 3 and Tom at loose-head, because technically he was excellent in that practice game and we thought he could do a job against Julian White. But we didn't announce Tom in our team for the final. We waited until ninety minutes before kick-off and I remember Cockerill going berserk because they'd obviously planned to have a go at our front row, but with Vickery on the other side now and French coming in, it was going to be completely different. On the day, Frenchy was brilliant and our scrum held together fantastically well.'

Out-thought off the field and eventually out-fought on it, this was not Leicester's day. It was a trophy they thoroughly earned, too, because Wasps's route to the final had been less than clear-cut. Drawing crack French sides Perpignan and Castres in their pool had been daunting enough and, after losing to Perpignan in round two, McGeechan's side had travelled to Castres in January for their final game needing a win to top the pool, otherwise their hopes might have ended there and then.

Saluting a tremendous, backs-to-the-wall 16–13 win, solidly founded on the tireless heroics of flanker Joe Worsley and Lawrence Dallaglio's leadership, then *Daily Telegraph* rugby correspondent Brendan Gallagher opined: 'Wasps have flattered to deceive occasionally this season but it is time to dish out a large dollop of mid-season praise. Playing in a

RIGHT Alesana Tuilagi of Leicester Tigers is tackled by opposing winger Paul Sackey.

BELOW Leicester centre Ollie Smith sends a pass along the line.

ABOVE Lawrence Dallaglio leads the Wasps celebrations with the Heineken Cup trophy.

pool containing not one but two top French sides, they have emerged as the competition's second seeds. You can't ask for much more . . . a tremendous all-round effort, which ranks with anything they have achieved in Europe before.'

High praise indeed. And Wasps were imperious in the knock-out stages, hammering Irish giants Leinster 35–13 in High Wycombe before going on to record an equally comprehensive 30–13 semi-final victory over relegation-bound Northampton, thus setting the scene for Twickenham.

For McGeechan, renowned for his work with the British & Irish Lions, winning this Heineken Cup final against Leicester is right up there with his finest coaching achievements. Thirteen years on, he says: 'I'd put the 1997 Lions win in South Africa, Scotland's 1990 Grand Slam and winning the European Cup in 2007 as my top three memories, with Wasps being my top club experience. It was a huge moment in my career. I'd been at Northampton for five years and we'd always targeted to win the Heineken Cup, but I'd gone back to coach Scotland the year before Saints won it in 2000 so it was extra nice finally to win it with Wasps. What made it so special was the feeling with the crowd, the flags, the atmosphere and knowing we'd prepared our tactics really well. At club level, I'd always wanted to win Europe because it means all the other teams are second to you.'

For Wasps, however, things would never be quite the same again. Sure, they eked out a fourth Premiership title in six years against Leicester in 2008, but that match was Dallaglio's last before retiring and with the old guard disappearing at a rate of knots, the decline set in.

Saracens and Harlequins were the growing forces in London and, amid a backdrop of mounting debt and declining crowds at their remote stadium in High Wycombe, relegation to the second division was only narrowly avoided in 2012. As then director of rugby Dai Young later conceded, had London Wasps not retained their Premiership status at that time, it would have been curtains.

But new money was found and, in October 2014, Wasps took the unprecedented step of removing 'London' from their name and decamping to Coventry, where they now train in the city and play at the Ricoh Arena. However you wish to dress it up, the old Wasps we knew no longer exists and twelve years have now elapsed since the club claimed its last silverware – almost unthinkable when Dallaglio & Co. were dominating domestic rugby and rampaging their way around Europe.

For this correspondent, the Heineken Cup win over Leicester in 2007 remains a special memory.

South Africa and Wales Celebrate

EDDIE BUTLER

I t was a rugby season totally lacking in serenity, a long haul of many contrasts and much hysteria. It probably won't be recognised anywhere as a vintage year for style, but, goodness, it generated some drama. Even South Africa, the team crowned world champions as early as 20 October 2007, defied their aversion to risk on the field by playing a full part in the season's general mayhem.

The Springboks came to the sixth Rugby World Cup without great expectation, it seemed, and without any desire to play their way into contention through adventure. In short, they kicked the leather off the ball. They sacrificed width for height, the abiding memory of their winning formula being Butch James and Frans Steyn hammering the ball into the sky.

Boom and chase. It was the chosen method of the other success story of that World Cup – Argentina. Juan Martín Hernández had almost exactly the same routine, the only difference being that he, smoothness personified, kicked upwards with a graceful stroke, as against the bludgeon of Butch's boot. The two met in the semi-final and something apart from the seam on the poor ball had to give. In the end it was Argentina who yielded (13–37), but they immediately recovered and beat France for the second time (having upset the hosts in the very first game of the tournament) in the third–fourth final. Yes, the simple art of kicking had its rewards.

That double-defeat of the hosts was part of the less straightforward nature of the season. France under coach Bernard Laporte never enjoyed unquestioningly loyal home support at their own World Cup. The first pool defeat to Argentina seemed to trigger a probe into all that was supposedly wrong with French rugby. For starters, it meant France, instead of playing a quarter-final at home, now had to leave their own land to play New Zealand in Cardiff. What sort of French World Cup was that?

France, of course, proceeded to beat the All Blacks and delirium briefly elbowed self-loathing the way of New Zealand. To be frank, the defeat didn't go down well there. Had the All Blacks forgotten how to drop a goal? This was a question much more politely put than the ones asked in fury at the time of the 20–18 defeat of referee Wayne Barnes's eyesight and parentage.

Now back home, forgiven France's stay of damnation was short. Having beaten New Zealand against all the odds in Wales, they now slumped to England in the semi-final in Paris. And when they lost to Argentina in the minor final, that probe into

BELOW The controversial France/All Blacks quarter-final began with a seriously confrontational eyeball-to-eyeball *haka*.

ABOVE Christophe Dominici of France is tackled by Frederico Martin Aramburú of Argentina during the Bronze Final of Rugby World Cup 2007. Aramburú scored one of Argentina's five tries in their 34–10 victory.

RIGHT Springbok full-back Percy Montgomery landed four out of four penalty attempts during the World Cup final. Frans Steyn kicked South Africa's other three points.

Bernard Laporte's allegedly murky life – in rugby, in his many business dealings and in the political world to which he aspired – made a front-page splash. The ball was heavily kicked at the 2007 World Cup, but so was the French coach when he was down.

For England it was a very different story. Having won the World Cup in 2003, it is no exaggeration to say that they had right-royally fallen off their pedestal. They came to France both as defending champions and pretty rank outsiders. In the pool stages they met South Africa and were smashed mercilessly, 36–0. But from then on, England pulled themselves together. In the quarter-final in Marseille, they beat Australia. And in the semi, they did for France.

Meanwhile, the Springboks had celebrated victory over England by making eleven changes and nearly losing (30–25) to Tonga. The day after England beat Australia in Marseille, South Africa faced Fiji in the same place and captain John Smit had to gather his Springboks around him and issue a few home-truths: 'Carry on like this and we're out.' The pack rallied and the kicking boots went back to work and South Africa won 37–20.

ABOVE Butch James of South Africa is tackled by England full-back Jason Robinson, try-scorer in the 2003 final.

RIGHT Jonny Wilkinson tackles J. P. Pietersen. For all the team's kicking, right wing Pietersen and Bryan Habana on the left meant that South Africa had plenty of pace available out wide.

Now, in the final, England and South Africa met again. 2007 wasn't quite such a topsy-turvy year that England managed to beat the favourites (they lost 6–15), but had it not been for the faintest brush of the touchline by the knee of Mark Cueto then they might well have come out ahead. Part of the strangeness of the season was that England so very nearly mounted a successful defence of their world title.

No World Cup tribulations – not even France's or New Zealand's – compared with Wales's. Gareth Jenkins's squad didn't exactly go to France as favourites to win the tournament, but with the most peculiar gift of home advantage (in Cardiff, that is) for their pool games against Australia and Japan, they were fully expected to reach the last eight. That meant, after defeat to Australia, having to defeat Fiji at the Stade Beaujoire in Nantes in the last pool game.

It was an extraordinary encounter, which will come as no consolation to the Welsh, who lost 38–34. Japan are responsible for three (*vs* South Africa in 2015 and *vs* Ireland then Scotland in 2019) of the four World Cup games that keep alive the prospect of rugby stretching beyond its traditional citadels, but Fiji–Wales had a

ABOVE Veteran England scrum-half Andy Gomarsall moves the ball away from the base of a ruck during the final.

The Welsh renaissance forms the second half of the story of this season. The World Cup of 2007 played its part and now came the Six Nations of 2008. In between there was the cruel formality of dismissing Gareth Jenkins, a sad end to a pioneering career with Llanelli and the Scarlets. Only with that abrupt cessation could the era of Warren Gatland begin.

majesty all of its own. With it came total adoration for the way Fiji play rugby; without it there would have been no subsequent Welsh revival and renaissance of their own unique way of playing the game.

The new coach came in from his home province of Waikato, NZ, but he brought in assistants with whom he had recently worked at Wasps. Rob Howley brought a serious, technical study of plays with him; Shaun Edwards brought a bellowing intensity that knocked a genuinely talented but mutinous team into line. Whatever bolshiness had manifested itself against the coaching regimes of Mike Ruddock in 2006 and Gareth Jenkins in 2007, there was no argument about who was now the boss. The previous captain, Gareth Thomas, was eased out of the door and Gatland named Ryan Jones as the new leader of twelve of the number 8's Ospreys team-mates (only Mark Jones and Martyn Williams played elsewhere) for the first game of the championship, against England away.

England led 16–6 at half-time, playing as formidably as they had in full recovery-mode at the World Cup. It was not looking promising for Wales, but somehow England started to unravel in the second half and went from being consummately in control to haphazard in the extreme. Wales scored twenty points in thirteen minutes and that was that.

Two consecutive home games and wins, against Scotland and Italy, opened up all sorts of possibilities that the new coaching team refused point-blank to discuss, but which the rest of Wales could not help but debate non-stop. Everything hinged on a difficult encounter with Ireland at Croke Park in Dublin, which included the return of Gatland to the country he had once coached . . . and about which he had memories that were not always of the fondest. The process of settling a few scores started then and would continue until he departed after the World Cup of 2019. In fact, this was more than just about scores; this was the start of a feud and probably did as much to drive up standards of play as any technical novelties introduced along the coach's twelve-year way with Wales.

On that day, Shane Williams, fast cementing his place as an all-time favourite, scored a try and Wales won by four points, setting up the finale against France in Cardiff. This Grand Slam opportunity was less fraught than the away games – Wales at home in round 5 with the biggest domestic prize up for grabs tend to seize the moment. It was the first of their three Grand Slams and their four titles under Warren Gatland. A season that had swayed and plunged ended with composure and wild celebration.

'If Only': The Tale of the 2009 Lions

MICK CLEARY

There are many snapshots that capture the essence of the 2009 British and Irish Lions tour to South Africa: the schoolboy innocence of pre-tour assembly at Pennyhill Park, all wonder and hope; the media sit-down with Dr James Robson at Umhlanga Rocks prior to the First Test with the good doctor expressing amazement that there was almost an entire complement fit for training (famous last words); the sorrow on Phil Vickery's face as he trudged from the field in that opening Test in Durban after a mauling from Tendai 'The Beast' Mtawarira, regret in every syllable later to be uttered when the prop spoke to the press some ten days after his match-shaping ordeal; or the sickening line-up of Lions casualties as they piled into the ambulance after the brutally gripping Second Test at Loftus Versfeld. All of these images captured the mood of the moment and told a tale. But the most resonant of all was the sight of several Lions players trooping back into their Pretoria hotel having turned around en route to some much-deserved R and R following that Second Test. They couldn't face it. The series may have been lost. But they were not going to cut and run. They were not going to hide away. They were all in this together.

That phrase should serve as the mantra of the 2009 tour. In itself, the phrase does not sound particularly remarkable. Every team should express a sense of unity. But this was different. The Lions are different. They are made up of four constituent parts, often fractious parts, rivals for the most part, foes even. The key aspect in 2009 was that the Lions ethos had been undermined and diminished by the two preceding tours – to Australia in 2001 under Graham Henry followed by Clive Woodward's ill-constructed venture to New Zealand four years afterwards. Henry himself admitted a few years later that he had got it horribly wrong, deciding on his Test team almost prior to departure, while

BELOW Bryan Habana steps inside Ugo Monye of the Lions during the First Test, in Durban on 20 June 2009.

Woodward threw every last resource at beating the All Blacks, different coaching teams, split camps, hosts and hosts of players, all to the detriment of the all-important philosophy articulated above – a sense of tightness and camaraderie.

The 2009 Lions tour did not yield the desired results in the Test series but it delivered in every other way. Players loved it, fans loved it, coaches loved it, a unified view shared in the media. The Lions management had put a lot of work into making sure that the traditional values of tours should be restored.

McGeechan trimmed the tour party to thirty-seven and nominated a single coaching group – himself, Warren Gatland, Shaun Edwards, Rob Howley and Graham Rowntree. If there was a Wasps feel to it all, McGeechan made no apology for that even though he and the London club were to go their separate ways just before the tour started.

The captain was an Irishman, Munster lock Paul O'Connell, very much in the mould of the man

McGeechan as coach, on his fourth tour of duty as head honcho, and Gerald Davies as manager, with the backing of the Lions committee, set out to ensure that the trip upheld all the qualities of tours in the past – namely, that every single player had a fair crack at getting a Test spot, that players mixed in together, sharing rooms, playing three times in eight days if injury struck and being loyal to each other and to the cause.

chosen by McGeechan twelve years earlier when Martin Johnson led the first Lions party of the professional era. McGeechan realised back then the essential truth of touring South Africa, one he had seen at first hand as a player on the famous '99 call' tour of 1974, that a hard, physical edge has to be there at every turn. O'Connell, who got the nod ahead of his countryman and 2005 captain, Brian O'Driscoll, was the essence of that style: big of stature and whole-hearted of approach. O'Connell was also a straight-talker. The Munsterman had started all three Tests in New Zealand four years earlier. Big things had been expected of him in a Martin Johnson sort of role. Yet it didn't happen. O'Connell did not try to varnish the truth as the squad gathered under his leadership for the 2009 tour to South Africa.

'It is about doing justice to the Lions jersey,' said O'Connell. 'A lot of us didn't do it justice in 2005.'

The tone was set. The schedule was tight with just six games prior to the First Test at King's Park. The Lions battled and scuffed their way to victory in some of those matches, surviving a jittery, altitude-afflicted opener in Rustenburg to win what should have been a gentle loosener but turned out to be anything but as they came from 25–13 down to register a crucial first win, 37–25. On the same day, the Bulls showed the strength of rugby in South Africa when taking the 2009 Super Rugby title, beating Waikato Chiefs by an emphatic 61–7. 'It was all a good kick up the backside for us,' reflected Phil Vickery of a salutary opening weekend.

The Lions were soon on their mettle, dispatching the Golden Lions 74–10 in their next game and continuing in that feisty vein all the way through to the Test series, impressing at times with the flow of their

BOTTOM LEFT Springboks replacement
Jaque Fourie scores the third Springbok
try of the Second Test despite the tackle
of Tommy Bowe,

RIGHT Ronan O'Gara's rash 80th-minute
tackle on Fourie du Preez that gave the
Springboks their series-winning penalty
chance.

BELOW RIGHT (*From left*) Schalk Burger,
Bakkies Botha and Andries Bekker of
South Africa celebrate their series win
after the Second Test.

rugby but also showing that they could fight their way out of a tight corner if they needed to. Played six, won six, the first unbeaten Lions at this juncture since the 1989 tourists to Australia. They were in good shape. But then so too were the South Africans, world champions two years earlier and hot-shots in Super Rugby.

What ensued was the most compelling, enthralling and brutal two Tests that many of us have ever witnessed, an examination of character as much as it was of skill and resilience. Hindsight is only ever in the gift of the tour chronicler not in the hands of the management of the day. But the sight of a ruddy-faced, bowed Vickery told a sorry story, namely that Adam Jones should have started on the tighthead. And to judge by the manner in which Simon Shaw rose to the challenge in the Second Test, it should have been the Wasps man packing down alongside O'Connell at King's Park.

Instead, it was advantage Springboks almost from the first whistle, captain John Smit, burrowing through for a try in the fifth minute. The Lions never did recover their equilibrium even if they gave the 'Boks a fright as they recovered from a 26–7 deficit just after half-time to close to within five points at the final whistle at 26–21.

If you wanted to clutch at straws as a Lions fan then you would be buoyed by the performance in the second half. But the scoreboard had a damning ring to it nonetheless. There was now no margin for error. The Lions had come back from losing the opening Test in 1989 to claim the spoils in Australia but it was a daunting task. The Lions felt that they would improve and certainly there were likely to be changes in selection. But any

BELOW Jamie Heaslip is tackled by Ruan Pienaar and Ryan Kankowski (*right*) of South Africa during the Third Test, won 9–28 by the Lions. Note the position of Kankowski's hand.

optimism was offset by the knowledge that the Springboks would also get better. And the game was in Pretoria.

Loftus Versfeld is the spiritual home of South African rugby. It is where the hard-core Afrikaner fans feel most at home. They were certainly in the mood for battle on a typically splendid blue-sky winter's afternoon on the high veldt. The press box at Loftus is behind glass. I opted for an overspill seat out among the diehards, among the few places usually given over to Pretoria Police reservists. They made room for me, just.

The tone was set right from the start when Schalk Burger tussled over the touchline with Lions' wing Luke Fitzgerald. The Irishman was gouged, an act of violence that was right under the nose of touch-judge Bryce Lawrence. For some inexplicable reason, the New Zealander ducked his responsibility and advised only a yellow card. Referee Christophe Berdos had not seen the incident so only ten minutes in the sin-bin it was for the Springbok back-row forward. On that decision turned so much.

The Lions did take initial advantage with full-back Rob Kearney, one of five changes, crossing for a try. The Lions were far more proactive, far more assertive than they had been at King's Park, as well they knew that they needed to be. 'South Africa have a bullying mentality and we have to get in their faces,' forwards coach Warren Gatland had said.

Shaw was immense and it made you wonder why it had taken seventeen appearances for the Lions in twelve years before he was entrusted with a starting spot. But for all the mighty efforts up front, there were still lapses of concentration. J. P. Pietersen was allowed through too easily and even though the Lions led, 16–8, at the half-time break, they were far from being in clear water.

Calamity struck at the start of the second-half when they lost both props, Gethin Jenkins and Adam Jones, to injury. Later, their two centres, Jamie Roberts and Brian O'Driscoll, were also to leave the field. Bryan Habana got a try for South Africa, the respective boots kept swinging and as the clock ticked down, it looked as if the Lions had done enough.

If only . . . Ronan O'Gara had kicked to touch rather than back upfield. If only O'Gara had not followed up his clearance with a wild mid-air challenge on Fourie de Preez. If only Morné Steyn had not been such a prodigious kicker and the series-winning penalty had not sailed over from inside his own half.

If only . . . The refrain of the 2009 British and Irish Lions tour of South Africa

Leicester's Finest Premiership

PAUL BOLTON

2009-2010

Ten years may seem a lifetime to Leicester Tigers supporters who have grown frustrated at seeing their side toothless near the bottom of the Premiership table in recent years, but not so long ago the date for the competition finale at Twickenham was inked into diaries alongside the city's traditional July holiday fortnight.

Leicester reached the final in nine consecutive seasons from 2005 to 2013, winning the title four times with their most recent success coming in the last of those appearances against Northampton Saints. The third, and most exhilarating of those wins came in the 2010 final when Leicester beat Saracens 33–27 with a late converted try from Dan Hipkiss after the title appeared to be heading to Saracens when Glen Jackson had landed a seventy-sixth minute penalty to nudge them a point in front.

Hipkiss's try gave Leicester back-to-back titles following a 10–9 win over London Irish at Twickenham in 2009 but, with the obvious benefit of hindsight, it is clear that Tigers were coming towards the end of a glorious period of success and that challenges to their domination were coming from other quarters.

Saracens avenged their defeat in the 2011 final when they beat Leicester 22–18 to win the Premiership for the first time. Four more titles – plus an extra-time defeat by Northampton in the 2014 final – followed before Saracens' success was tarnished by being caught with their fingers in the salary cap till.

Leicester, in contrast, have lost the recipe that brought them so much success and have spent long years searching in vain for it. Richard Cockerill, a pillar of their pack for so many years and a key member of the coaching staff throughout the period, was sacked on New Year's Day 2017 but there has been no discernible improvement in performances or fortunes under Aaron Mauger, Matt O'Connor or Geordan Murphy.

Murphy, like Cockerill, was a fans' favourite during an illustrious playing career which included seven Premiership titles and the Leicester captaincy. That record may have helped Murphy to buy more time when he was moved into a new role as director of rugby, leaving Steve Borthwick with the task of leading Leicester's coaching team after five years as England's forwards' coach. Murphy, however, left the club later in 2020.

BELOW Saracens scrum-half Neil de Kock is tackled by his opposite number Ben Youngs (right) and centre Anthony Allen during the 2010 Guinness Premiership final.

ABOVE Petrus du Plessis is tackled by Lewis Moody of Leicester.

RIGHT Toby Flood landed four out of six penalty attempts during the final as well as converting all three Leicester tries.

A change of coach usually requires patience from supporters while players adapt to a new voice and allow different systems to bed in. But, as Mauger discovered when he was discarded the day after Leicester won the Anglo Welsh Cup in March 2017, patience tends to wear thin rather quickly at Welford Road.

At least Leicester supporters have plenty of fond memories to sustain them through the more challenging recent times, none more so than the euphoria that followed Hipkiss's last-gasp try in 2010. Borthwick, who was replaced in the Saracens' pack early in the second half, collected a runners-up medal.

The winning score was the result of hard, monotonous work on the Oval Park training pitch

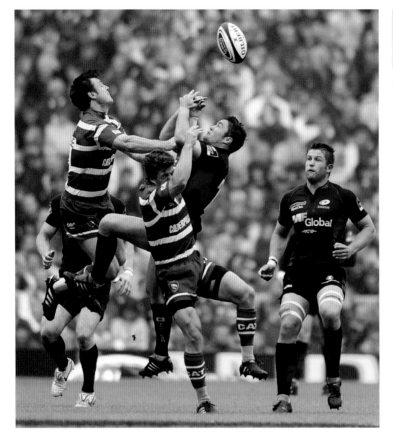

'We're boring and we train every day. We work hard on the training field,' Cockerill said afterwards. 'You don't win kick-offs at the end and you don't steal line-outs at the end by luck. It's from hard work. I wondered how we would get the ball back, but Floody kicked it in the right spot, Scott Hamilton caught it, Danny Hipkiss finished it off and we won the game.'

where Leicester had rehearsed the scenario of winning back possession after going behind to a late score.

Toby Flood's well-judged restart kick was snaffled by wing Scott Hamilton. The former All Black then made ground before he off-loaded to replacement centre Hipkiss whose progress appeared to have been halted by Saracens before they suddenly obligingly parted and allowed him to untangle himself from a tackle and break free for the try which Flood duly converted.

Flood had booted Leicester to a less entertaining and nerve-shredding victory over Bath in the semi-final at Welford Road where he landed five penalties to Olly Barkley's two in a try-less contest.

Saracens had finished third in the regular season and edged out second-placed Northampton 21–19 in their semi-final at Franklin's Gardens which proved to be a nice dress-rehearsal for an outstanding final.

In the final the accurate Glen Jackson – later to become an international referee – nudged Saracens ahead with two penalties, Flood pulled one back before Matt Smith, who was replaced by Hipkiss, went over from a crisp handling move, with Hamilton delivering the scoring pass. Saracens responded with a superb try of their own, a patient and sustained attack which saw Jackson and Jacques Burger send skipper

Ernst Joubert over for the first of two tries. Saracens were found wanting in defence, though, when Ben Youngs stole through a gap and gave Leicester a 20–14 lead at half-time.

After the break, Joubert was in the right place again to finish off another thrilling Saracens attack with centre Adam Powell making the initial break and openside flanker Andy Saull creating space with a deft off-load as he rode a tackle. Flood gave Leicester some breathing space when he landed another penalty but Jackson held his nerve to land two in quick succession to put Saracens within touching distance of victory. But Hamilton stole the restart from under the noses of Hugh Vyvyan and Petrus du Plessis, he then cut infield and Hipkiss, playing his first match in more than three months having recovered from an ankle injury, burst through a maul when seemingly held by Jackson and powered over.

There was still time for Saracens to mount a final attack but Geoff Parling stole a line-out on Leicester's 22 from the final play of the match and Ben Youngs hoofed the ball into the East Stand seats to start the celebrations.

Elsewhere in the 2009/10 season there was a Grand Slam for France in the Six Nations which included a 33–10 thumping of Ireland at the Stade de France, which scuppered Ireland's hopes of a second consecutive Grand Slam.

England stuttered under manager Martin Johnson, who was unable to transfer success as a captain into international coaching. England managed only an unconvincing victory over Argentina in their three autumn internationals and laboured through the Six Nations after a comfortable opening round victory over Wales at Twickenham. England won only narrowly (17–12) in Rome, lost to Ireland at Twickenham and drew 15–15 at Murrayfield before making France work hard for a 12–10 win and the Grand Slam in Paris.

New Zealand reclaimed the Tri Nations title they had surrendered to South Africa in 2009 by winning all six of their matches, their fourth Grand Slam and their tenth title. New Zealand also retained the IRB Women's Rugby World Cup although hosts England pushed them hard before going down 13–10 in the final at the Twickenham Stoop. The win extended the Black Ferns' unbeaten run in the competition to nineteen consecutive matches following defeat by the United States in the 1991 semi-finals.

There was a landmark first title for Samoa in the IRB World Sevens Series where they won three consecutive tournaments during February and March and four of the last five including the series decider at Murrayfield. Captain Lolo Lui landed a drop-goal in extra time to secure a dramatic semi-final victory over England and the points Samoa required to claim the crown.

Ospreys became the first side to win the Magners League for the third time and they did it the hard way with a 17–12 win over Leinster on their own patch at the RDS. Toulouse defeated Biarritz in all-French affair in the Heineken Cup final in Paris but Cardiff Blues became the first Welsh side to win a European title with a 28–21 victory over Toulon in the Challenge Cup final in Marseille.

BELOW Leicester players celebrate their 33–27 victory at the final whistle.

The First Major Win for Saracens

HUGH GODWIN

The 2010/11 season for Saracens ended with the first Premiership title of their five to date, to which they have added three European Cups, but where did it begin? In the airport lounge on that year's team-bonding trips to Miami and the Munich beer festival? Or in the offices of the South Africans whose interest and investment in 2008 breathed life into a club becoming synonymous with falling short of the big prizes? It was, most authentically, surely the November evening in 1995 when Nigel Wray was sold control of Saracens' name and first-division status and set out on a quarter of a century and counting of transforming an amateur team with a tiny grandstand on a council-owned pitch into the most discussed and divisive and second-most trophy-laden English club of the open era.

I bore witness to some of the above events as I have always lived close to Saracens and their various home stadiums and training grounds around north London, while others such as the Miami trip in April 2011 – a mix of eye-opening practice sessions at the facilities of the Dolphins American football team, and barbecues and beers and driving the highways in half a dozen RVs – have been passed on as folklore by the players. I stood in the tiny office doubling as a press room after the match in 1995 at which Wray laid out the future he envisaged for the club, and it included night matches with Toulouse in the European Cup – and if anyone there says they didn't raise a sceptical eyebrow, they are not telling you the truth.

In fact it all came to pass – apart from the bit where Wray pictured those matches at the club's then home at Bramley Road, where before kick-off the players used to clear the mess left by dog-walkers – but it was not a smooth or exponential path, and 2010/11 stands as a season of crucial breakthrough as the team who beat Leicester 22–18 in the Premiership Final at Twickenham on 28 May 2011 delivered some long-

TOP James Short of Saracens scores the first try of the 2011 Premiership final despite the attentions of Scott Hamilton of Leicester.

TOP Petrus du Plessis of Saracens is tackled by George Skivington (5) and Thomas Waldrom of Leicester Tigers.

RIGHT Saracens coach Andy Farrell tosses a kicking tee to son Owen Farrell during the final. Owen had a 100 per cent success rate with the boot in the match, five penalties and a conversion.

awaited company for the Tetley's Bitter Cup of 1998 in the Saracens trophy cabinet.

Leicester were the reigning champions, and nine times winners since the English leagues began in 1987, and in the last knockings of the final they hammered at Saracens' goal-line through thirty-two nerve-jangling phases of rucks, earned a penalty and went through another half-dozen phases before Owen Farrell leapt forward to tackle his opposite number, the England fly-half Toby Flood, and put the attack to an end. The year before, when the same clubs contested the final, Leicester had exulted in a late winning try.

This was Saracens version 2.0 – a mix of South Africans who had arrived as part of the new investors' original idea of appealing to rugby-mad ex-pats in London, plus emerging young Englishmen and a quiet Ulsterman named Mark McCall hardly anyone was talking about yet. The director of rugby in the early part of the 2010/11 season was Brendan Venter, the former Springbok centre and present-day GP in Cape Town, who had been banned from the 2010 final for arguing with spectators in a league match at Leicester. By January 2011, Venter was repositioned as technical director, making occasional visits from South Africa, while the day-to-day influencers were McCall as Venter's successor, Wray as the chairman and spiritual overseer, and Edward Griffiths, the influential ideas man and chief executive. It was Griffiths and Venter who urged the need for a holistic, more wholesome approach to the playing squad. Buying big names, as Wray had done from the outset, was not an answer in itself, and Saracens version 1.0 had only got so far with the likes of François Pienaar, Philippe Sella, Michael Lynagh, Tim Horan and Thomas Castaignède among many a star name.

'It had been a club where it seemed money was the most important thing,' Griffiths said in September 2020. 'We switched the focus to looking after them better than anyone else – whether that was preparing them for second careers after rugby or looking after their wives and families. It was an attempt to pull together people who were prepared to try unbelievably hard and would be treated unbelievably well.'

This approach was later determined to have bent the rules of the Premiership's salary cap but in 2010/11 it worked like magic, and the key figures in the final were highly significant. The nineteen-year-old Farrell had come as a package with his father, Andy – initially an injury-prone player signed in 2005; then as head coach alongside assistants Paul Gustard, Alex Sanderson and Dan Vickers – and the junior 'Faz' was a fresh-faced, floppy-haired fly-half, largely playing the game in the way he was directed. Alex Goode was a 23-year-old from Cambridge, in Saracens' traditional Eastern Counties contact area, who had come through the club's academy. Schalk Brits, the ever-smiling hooker, and Brad Barritt, the defensive rock of a centre, had arrived from Western Province and Natal respectively.

Saracens came into the Premiership final with twelve straight wins, and they had beaten Leicester home and away in the regular-season league meetings. I was working for a Sunday newspaper in those days, so tended to be present only at Sarries' Saturday matches, which initially had not been going so well. I saw them lose to London Irish in the opening weekend's 'London double-header' at Twickenham in September, and then away to Clermont Auvergne and to Leinster at Wembley in the European Cup on successive Saturdays in October. During the latter match, the South African fly-half Derick Hougaard ruptured an Achilles tendon, and Saracens signed Gavin Henson but the unpredictable Welshman had not played for nineteen months and was busy

With the former England captain Steve Borthwick at the heart of the pack, and an iron defence restricting the opposition to fifteen points at the most during that twelve-match winning sequence, Saracens edged Gloucester by 12–10 in a tense semi-final, with four penalty goals by Farrell.

honing his ballroom skills for the TV programme *Strictly Come Dancing*. Henson never fitted into the Saracens way, and his influence was minimal, unlike Goode, who was thrust to the fore by Hougaard's season-ending injury. Farrell had been on loan at Bedford, then ill with appendicitis, but he was ever present from November onwards, and gradually took over the goal-kicking from Goode, who reverted to full-back.

While Griffiths, Wray and their South African colleagues were quietly exploring options for a new stadium instead of sharing at Watford FC, I was invited in April 2011 to report on Goode doing work experience at Allianz, a club sponsor, in the City of London. The Rugby Players Association said Saracens were 'ahead of the game' with forty of their forty-nine-man squad gaining meaningful work experience or running their own business or in formal study or education. David Priestley, who was running the programme for the club, said: 'I won't rest until it is 100 per cent.' Players practised their public speaking and did 'speed-date' networking sessions with chief executives. They were addressed by high-achieving sportspeople including Sir Jackie Stewart from Formula One, the cricketer Justin Langer and the boxer Billy Schwer. 'It makes players emotionally more rounded and resilient,' Priestley told me. 'It smooths out the highs and lows of winning and losing, and freshens them up for training.'

The prevailing feeling was the self-styled 'Men in Black' had played too freely in the 2010 final. 'Maybe they've learnt their lesson,' Flood of Leicester said beforehand. 'To do what they need to do to win the game, rather than do what it needs to look good.'

Still, the only Saracens try of the 2011 final, in the twelfth minute, was swift and brave. Goode took a quick line-out, Brits went hitch-kicking on a diagonal run, and James Short scored at the left corner. Flood was outdone in the battle of the kickers, as Farrell – who was making his Twickenham debut – converted all six of his shots at goal, while the much more experienced Tiger missed from around 40 metres, on shallow angles, after 52 and 55 minutes when Leicester trailed 19–12 and needed points. Flood also fluffed a penalty kick to touch after 58 minutes, and when he forced the pace with the ball in hand, getting his arms through the tackle,

Saracens knew it was coming and batted the ball from his grasp. Flood recovered with a pair of penalties either side of one by Farrell in the final quarter but the damage was done. Farrell repeatedly had to pause on Saracens' lap of honour to stretch his cramping calves but the smile never left him or his team-mates from the workaholic number 8 Ernst Joubert to the English-American outside centre Chris Wyles, and the recently recruited prop Matt Stevens to Namibia's finest – the ferocious tackler, Jacques Burger.

'To come here to this special place and do it to a team like Leicester is unbelievable,' said Farrell, as the club song, 'Stand up for the Saracens' – rewritten as 'Stand for the Champions' in anticipation – blared out. The ditty, donated by Right Said Fred, was irritatingly catchy, as befitted a club that was questioning many of English rugby's hoary old habits, and now producing tangible answers.

LEFT Nigel Wray of Saracens celebrates with the Aviva Premiership trophy.

BELOW Saracens Director of Rugby Mark McCall leads the celebrations in the dressing room following the Premiership final.

Lancaster Restores English Pride

CHRIS JONES

Though aftermath of England's disastrous attempt to win the 2011 Rugby World Cup in New Zealand saw the departure of Martin Johnson as head coach and the arrival of the 'company man' as Stuart Lancaster was viewed. He was already on the Rugby Football Union payroll having been made the union's Head of Elite Player Development in 2008, a role that included coaching the England Saxons.

Having taken over the top role on an interim basis at the end of 2011, Lancaster went about rebuilding the England team from the bottom up. Back to basics was one theme, along with personal discipline and humility, making up important pillars of the system he wanted to create, and to help achieve this aim, he put his faith in a player who encapsulated the kind of rugby ethics that Lancaster wanted to employ.

That man was Chris Robshaw who had just one cap when appointed as captain for the first two matches of the 2012 Six Nations championship in a season that would see him lift the Premiership trophy as captain of Harlequins. Robshaw and Lancaster shared common values, believed that hard work and total commitment to the cause should be 'givens' for anyone selected for the national squad and there would be no time for prima donnas, dwarf-throwers or those who believed their longevity in the team gave them more wriggle room. The damaging lessons of the many mistakes made during the World Cup visit to Queenstown were learnt.

To many in the sport – particularly around the debris of the England senior team – the appointment of Lancaster was viewed as a sticking plaster, with the head coach job eventually going to go to someone like South Africa's Nick Mallett who had a proven international coaching pedigree. This, after all, was the head coach of the national team of the biggest and richest rugby nation in the world. A big job needed a big name. We were wrong.

Right from the start, Lancaster was inclusive, particularly when dealing with a media totally fed up with stories of misbehaving players. Powerpoint presentations – some off the record, others that could be reported – were staged by the shaven-headed Lancaster as he laid out the way forward he intended to plot for England. In truth, many of those sitting in the darkened room staring at the slides projected onto the screen, wondered if this was just pie in the sky, the plans of a man who was only going to be around for a short time.

Patently, Lancaster could give a very impressive presentation, but could he coach an international team?

Slowly, it became clear that the RFU had, remarkably, found in their own ranks, a coach who

LEFT Stuart Lancaster and Chris Robshaw at an England press conference before the autumn internationals later in 2012.

TOP RIGHT Richie Gray offloads as he is tackled by Chris Ashton (*left*) and Ben Foden in the 2012 Calcutta Cup, won 6–13 by England.

RIGHT Scrum-half Chris Cusiter of Scotland gets his pass away as Chris Robshaw tries to make the tackle.

ABOVE Wales number 8 Taulupe Faletau (*left*) and winger Alex Cuthbert tackle England's Manu Tuilagi during the 2012 Six Nations clash.

actually knew what the problems were with the national team; he was prepared to start from scratch and help regain the English rugby public's trust. His willingness to take action was highlighted when Harlequins scrum-half Danny Care was removed from the elite squad after he was charged with drink-driving. This action was taken against a player Lancaster knew extremely well from their days together in the Leeds academy, which the England head coach had run. Despite him knowing Care so well, there would be no 'special cases'.

Lancaster's new vision for England became clear when he announced his squad for the 2012 RBS Six Nations containing young, untried talent and missing many of the players who were at the World Cup. Of the 32 names included in the senior group, 15 were not in New Zealand with veterans Mike Tindall, Nick Easter and Mark Cueto shown the exit door. 'We want a leadership group that is strong,' explained Lancaster, whose coaching unit included Graham Rowntree and Andy Farrell. 'The ultimate aim is for the players to shape the culture and drive the programme. I always felt January 2012 was going to be a defining moment for the future.'

Amongst the new faces was Saracens' Owen Farrell, son of Andy, and clubmate Brad Barritt a no-nonsense centre with a strong defence and rock-hard attitude. They would make their England debuts against Scotland at Murrayfield in the opening match of the championship along with number 8 Phil Dowson. Farrell and Barritt became England's first uncapped centre pairing since 2002 – and only the second since 1969. Lancaster named

a total of eight uncapped players in his twenty-two-man squad for the trip to Murrayfield, with his starting line-up boasting just 236 Test caps, including Lions appearances, compared to Scotland's 501. The Scottish pack alone had more international experience than England.

Saracens fly-half Charlie Hodgson was the most experienced player on the England team sheet with 36 caps, but was making his first Test start in four years. It would be Hodgson who helped get the Lancaster era off to a winning start with a charge-down try which, allied to Farrell's kicks, saw England win 13–6 – their first success at Murrayfield in eight years. While England maintained their unbeaten record against Italy in Rome, a 19–15 win was a wake-up call against the weakest nation in the competition.

A bruising 19–12 loss to Wales featured a brilliant try saving tackle by Sam Warburton on the rampaging Manu Tuilagi and this would prove to be the result that meant England finished second – one of four times in a row under Lancaster that his team would be the bridesmaid in the tournament. Tuilagi's form was helping erase the image of him emerging from Auckland harbour having accepted a challenge from England team-mates to jump off a ferry coming into dock and reach land first. It was the last ludicrously reckless act of that 2011 World Cup squad.

Wins over France (24–22) in Paris – featuring a great solo try by Tuilagi who appeared to be treading water for the right reasons as he neared the line – and at home to Ireland (30–9) confirmed that England were back to being a team capable of making a real impact and in Farrell they had found an immediate Test-class kicking replacement for the retired Jonny Wilkinson.

The tangible reward for Lancaster was his confirmation as England's full-time head coach on 29 March, with the job of taking them to the 2015 Rugby World Cup that the RFU were hosting. Lancaster beat Mallett to the job and, having restored their standing in Europe, he then took his new-look squad to the Southern

ABOVE Geoff Parling is challenged by Eben Etzebeth during the Second Test, at Ellis Park, of England's 2012 tour. The Springboks won 36–27.

BOTTOM LEFT Toby Flood of England dives over for a try during the Second Test.

Hemisphere for a three-Test series against South Africa. Lancaster chided me with a reminder that I had described him as a 'sticking plaster' rather than the chosen man – but this rebuke was delivered with a friendly smile not a scowl. The head coach wasn't that kind of man.

The three tests with South Africa delivered two defeats and a 14–14 draw in Port Elizabeth with Harlequins's Joe Marler announcing himself on the international stage in the series. It was a reminder to Lancaster and his players that rugby monsters lurk below the Equator, capable of inflicting worrying defeats on the unwary and that injuries inevitably shape your planning. It was a salutary lesson at the end of a hectic and illuminating first international season for Lancaster that had seen him turn England from an international rugby embarrassment into a team capable of standing toe to toe with the best.

As his tenure unfolded, Lancaster's good humour and calmness in the most emotional of situations would be tested to the limit before it all came to a thoroughly disappointing end with England failing to make the knock-out stages of their own World Cup. However, in the wake of the South African tour, the feeling that England were back was inescapable.

The Day The Azzurri Beat Les Bleus

JOHN INVERDALE

2012-2013

When you're a freelance, asking for time off is never a good idea, but in 2000, I did indeed ask for the weekend off to go to Rome to see Italy's entrance into the Six Nations against Scotland. It had, after all, been ninety years since France had joined the party. This would be a once-in-a-lifetime moment as the most famous rugby tournament of all embraced the joy of six. And it was a truly unforgettable day. Diego Dominguez running the show from outside-half, and a gigantic swarm of a thousand Vespas hurtling round the streets outside the Stadio Flaminio to celebrate a famous Italian triumph that would signal a change in rugby's pecking order. Imagine Italy as Six Nations champions. One line that John Lennon strangely forgot to include.

Because here we are more than two decades later, still discussing whether the Azzurri merit their place in the competition. Should we have promotion and relegation? Should there be a second tier of the Six Nations (absolutely). When will South Africa turn six into seven? It seemed simpler in 2000 when trips to Rome were going to supplement the traditional weekends in Paris, Dublin or the British capital cities.

TOP Luciano Orquera evades the tackle of France hooker Dmitri Szarzewski. Orquera landed two conversions, a penalty and a drop goal during the match.

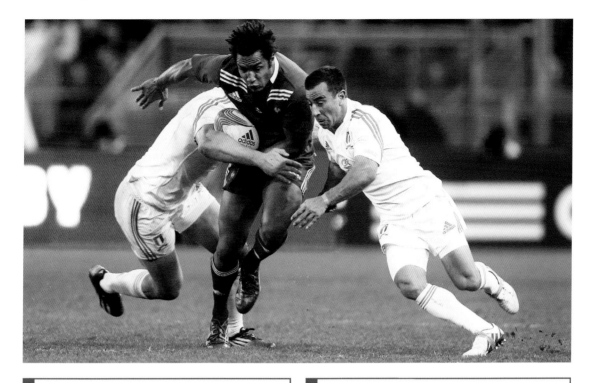

ABOVE Scorer of France's second try Benjamin Fall is tackled by Sergio Parisse (*left*) and Luciano Orquera.

BELOW Full-back Yoann Huget of France is tackled by Italy's hooker, Leonardo Ghiraldini.

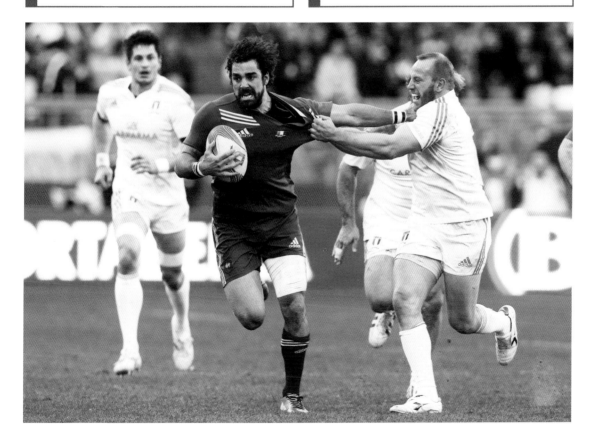

And there was one moment, in 2013, when all the false dawns, all the missed tackles, the perennial problems at half back, the 50- and 60- and 70-point drubbings, seemed like a bad memory. By that time, buoyed by an upturn in results and a belief that the quaint but dilapidated Flaminio was not a venue fit for Italian ambitions, the internationals had moved to the Stadio Olimpico. Italy had beaten France by a single point two years earlier, but Les Bleus had enjoyed a clean sweep in their autumn international campaign, and for the opening match of the Six Nations had a side full of household names, who were going to mount a serious challenge for the title. It wasn't a question of 'if' but of 'how many'.

Now one of the great mysteries, still unsolved, about Italian rugby, is why they have never been able to produce a play-making, ball-manipulating, prolific-kicking number 10, when the nation is more football obsessed than we are. How often have you seen Italy have a penalty forty metres out in front of the posts, and thought 'He'll miss this'; how often have you seen indecision, balls out on the full, intercept passes thrown, and thought 'I just don't get this'? When potential ambitions to play for Inter Milan or Juventus have been banished, why do those talented players, with hand and feet, not turn their attentions to the oval ball?

Anyway, that day in Rome, Luciano Orquera looked like he was the man. Now he'd been born in Argentina like Dominguez, but let's pass on that. For one glorious afternoon he orchestrated like Previn, danced like Nureyev, darted like Phil Taylor and kicked like Messi. Like a determined but startled rabbit he shot through the French defence early on to set up a try for Parisse in the days when the great number 8 still required occasional trips to the hairdresser. Even though Picamoles and Fall scored tries, the latter an absolute gem, and Michalak kicked goals to give France the lead, Luciano kept his cool. A lovely sniping run, somehow extricating himself from the grasp of two burly French forwards, and the pass found Martin Castrogiovanni – a man who rarely, if ever, went to a hairdresser. No one was going to stop Castro from five metres out.

After a further penalty, Italy led by five with the clock running down. Now there's nothing anti-France here, but you wanted them to hold out. To begin with a win and mount a challenge for the Six Nations for the first time. A yellow card for an Italian prop, a succession of five-metre scrums for France. You'd seen it all before. The try, the conversion, the narrow French win, the Italian heartbreak, the post-match 'We'll learn from this' interview, the analysis that under pressure they just couldn't hack it.

> **BELOW** Martin Castrogiovanni of Italy celebrates his try, which, when converted, gave Italy a 20–18 lead with twenty minutes remaining.

And then Benjamin Fall, scorer of such a sublime try earlier, was bundled into touch, and Nigel Owens blew the final whistle. And the Azzurri in white had beaten Les Bleus in blue, and it was bedlam. Parisse's unbridled joy would have tickled the Mona Lisa into

the tiniest of smiles. This was it. Italy, at last, on the way to being serious players.

There's the most brilliant sports bar, just off the Piazza del Popolo, more used to celebrating triumphs for Roma and Lazio and Valentino Rossi, which that

ABOVE Louis Picamoles, scorer of France's first try, is hauled down by Sergio Parisse in what would now be an illegal tackle, during Italy's marvellous 23–18 win, 3 February 2013.

night reverberated to the Italian anthem – surely the finest in the rugby world (with the possible exception of the Argentinan!). Watch out England. Watch out the All Blacks. Watch out world.

You know the rest. Italy won two matches that year, and France actually finished bottom of the table – that day in Rome the start of a ramshackle campaign. But for the Italians, at the time of writing on a horrible losing streak that runs to well over twenty Six Nations matches, it was another apparition of excellence. Orquera returned to life in the second violins after one majestic performance with the baton. And Parisse . . . well what can you say?

Sergio may mean Garcia to you, or it might mean Aguero. But to me, it will always mean the incomparable bulwark at the back of the Italian scrum. Taking the high ball from in front of his full-back's nose, fending off would-be assailants, flicking the ball nonchalantly out of the side of the hand, and even trying desperately to win matches with drop-goals from far out. And, OK, he was born in Argentina too. But he is pasta to Roberto Baggio's pizza. Italian to the core and as talismanic a sportsman as you can name. He didn't get the farewell he wanted at the Japan World Cup, and the stardust has peeled from his majestic body in recent years, but over the course of the twenty-five years of this book, can you name a more colossal player in European rugby?

I'd gone to the Eternal City in 2000 hoping to witness the start of something big in this sport. In 2013, there was a real glimpse that it might happen, though in many ways it now seems further away than ever. But I live in hope. Because rugby needs Italy.

There were obviously many other memories that year – a Lions' tour victory in Australia, and Wales' thirty-point drubbing of England in Cardiff spring to mind – but that day in Rome some of us thought we'd seen the future.

You may say I'm a dreamer. But I'm not the only one.

THE SARACENS FOUNDATION

THE SARACENS FOUNDATION IS THE CHARITABLE ARM OF SARACENS RUGBY CLUB.

WE TRANSFORM LIVES ON AND OFF THE PITCH TO BUILD STRONGER COMMUNITIES.

WE WORK COLLABORATIVELY TO ENHANCE THE EDUCATION, EMPLOYABILITY AND HEALTH OF OUR COMMUNITIES, TO BUILD A STRONGER AND MORE INCLUSIVE SOCIETY FOR ALL.

FIND OUT MORE ABOUT OUR WORK AND HOW YOU CAN SUPPORT US AT OUR WEBSITE, OR EMAIL FOUNDATIONINFO@SARACENS.NET

ABOVE Marland Yarde dives over to score the first try and opening points of the Second Test in the 7th minute.

RIGHT Ma'a Nonu scores New Zealand's third try in the 63rd minute, giving them a seemingly comfortable 28–13 lead.

It had been so near but yet so far for Lancaster's squad. Based on past experience, the expectation as they headed south was that the series would now become a one-sided ordeal. Local schoolchildren greeted England at Dunedin airport with an eyes-bulging *haka* and a local radio presenter dressed up in foliage and waited in the arrivals hall to poke fun at Billy Twelvetrees. It felt as if the host nation were joining forces to ram home their side's advantage after snatching a 1–0 lead.

But England did not roll over, in defiance of the expectations all around them. The line-up was reshuffled for the Second Test, staged at the Forsyth Barr Stadium – a futuristic indoor arena which many of the visiting players had experience of from 2011 World Cup pool matches at the venue. Manu Tuilagi was deployed on the wing, in an experiment which was not repeated.

Lancaster reintegrated a number of the Premiership finalists who had belatedly arrived on tour and also Billy Twelvetrees at inside centre, after the Gloucester playmaker had missed the series opener due to injury. The All Blacks again had a formidably powerful look and also the reassurance that they had blown away the cobwebs in Auckland, while managing to dodge an ambush.

The stage appeared to be set for a resounding New Zealand victory, but it didn't turn out that way. England led 10–6 at half-time, after an early try by Marland Yarde. At the start of the second half, they picked up where they had left off, taking the fight to the hosts before Twelvetrees – who had been highly effective and dangerous in midfield – threw a loose off-load which was pounced on by New Zealand, for a break-away try.

That was the tipping point, as Hansen's men located their higher gears and surged into a big lead. Again, an English surrender was anticipated. Again, it didn't come. Instead, they mounted a spirited, late rearguard action. Tries by Mike Brown and Chris Ashton brought the deficit back to just one point, but the visitors ran out of time to complete a sensational upset.

ABOVE Billy Twelvetrees in action for England during the Second Test, the only game he played on the tour.

It finished 28–27. Another near-miss. In a country where so many foreign teams are thrashed, England had gone toe-to-toe with the world's pre-eminent force and come close to beating them twice, on consecutive weekends. Instead, they were 2–0 down in the series, the Hillary Shield was back in Kiwi hands and a tough final week lay ahead, with only pride left to play for.

Before returning to the North Island, England made the short journey to Christchurch for what had become a rarity in modern times: a midweek game against provincial opposition. The Crusaders had real pedigree and the partisan local support was stirred into a pre-match frenzy by the pre-match show. But England played well, coped with the hostility and side-stepped a potential banana skin with ease, winning 38–7.

However, after moving on to Hamilton, the wheels came off the English chariot. The Red Rose squad were based in a low-grade, out-of-town hotel and the players were worn-out, cooped-up and cranky. It was a game too far. The Third Test was the sort of mismatch that the first two had been expected to be, as the All Blacks cruised to a 36–13 win on a wet and wild night at Waikato Stadium. Eastmond was hauled off at half-time, as the designated scapegoat, amid a frantic and vain attempt to plug a mass of defensive leaks. His Test career never really recovered; Burns and Ashton also disappeared into the international wilderness after that grim occasion – the former forever, the latter for four years.

All in all, it had been a proper tour, a proper challenge and – for the most part – a proper contest, which meant that the series was a successful and memorable event.

Until that capitulation, England had fronted up wonderfully well in the trying circumstances, at the end of a post-Lions season and without the ability to pick their best squad from the off. That ludicrous example of administrative self-harm would lead to protracted recriminations in the months after the tour. A degree of respect had been earned, where it hadn't existed before. Retallick and his team-mates grew to know the names of those Englishman who took them on, far from home, with considerable spirit. They also avoided controversies along the way, although the management's strict control over the squad did create simmering unrest below the surface, which would linger until the whole regime imploded at the 2015 World Cup.

Glasgow's Miles Better in the Pro12

ALAN LORIMER

In an attempt to promote Scotland's largest city as a location every bit as attractive as its more magnetic east coast rival, Edinburgh, some clever public relations bod came up with the simple but slick slogan: 'Glasgow's Miles Better'.

It may or may not have transformed overall perceptions of Scotland's west coast metropolis but when applied to rugby in the Clydeside city it rang true in May 2015 when Glasgow Warriors won the Pro12 Final. In doing so Warriors became the first Scottish professional club to scoop a major title of any variety. And in a football-mad city where Rangers and Celtic command acres of space in the sports pages, newspapers were suddenly forced to fire their clichéd hyperboles in a different direction.

As a Scot with an expectation of major rugby success about once every ten years, the Warriors' achievement is my outstanding memory of the 2014/15 season. Yet, it was not a title win that came out of the blue. Glasgow had been on an upward trajectory, under the direction of their inspirational coach, Gregor Townsend, who in 2012 had taken over from Sean Lineen as 'boss' at the Warriors.

Townsend's aim was to have his side playing at lightning pace to achieve a style that fitted his own view of the game and one akin to what he strove for in his own playing days. To that end he made some shrewd signings, not least a young fly-half by the name of Finn Russell, who had impressed for Scotland under-20s, despite not being first choice in the number 10 position at that age level.

Russell, who was awarded a full-time contract at Glasgow only at the start of the 2014/15 season, ultimately proved himself a winner, and not just in the final. It helped of course that he was surrounded by a stellar cast that included Stuart Hogg at full back, second rows Leone Nakarawa and Johnny Gray, and high scoring wingers Tommy Seymour and D. T. H. van der Merwe.

For much of the season it was another Fijian, Niko Matawalu, who lit up Friday nights at Scotstoun during the Pro12 campaign. Matawalu accumulated a string

> **ABOVE** Scrum-half Nikola Matawalu in action for Glasgow during the Pro12 semi-final with Ulster, 22 May 2015.

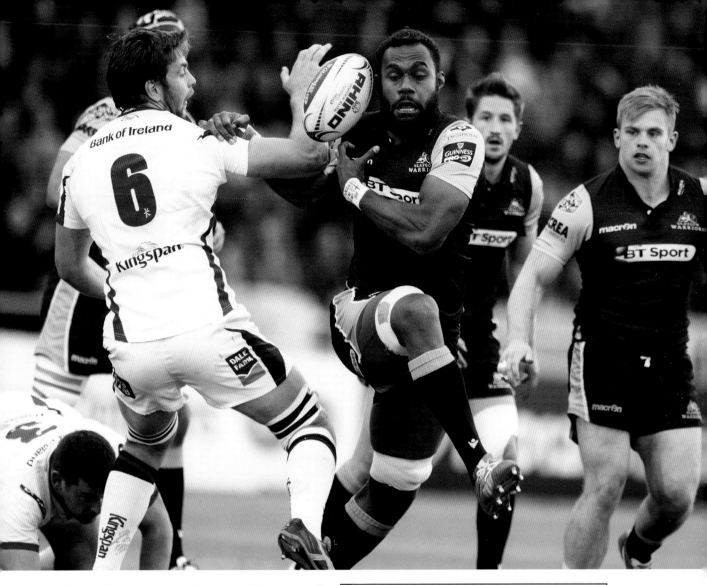

of man-of-the-match awards that made him a cult favourite among what was a growing following for the Warriors. The Fijian was one of the key players in helping to build Glasgow's momentum throughout the season, albeit his erratic play, brilliant one moment but costly the next, persuaded Townsend to leave him out of the starting team for the final. It was a calculated gamble but one which was ultimately vindicated.

Glasgow's results in the first half of the 2014/15 season, nine wins from eleven league games, were a pointer to Pro12 success for the Scotstoun club. Going into 2015, Warriors surprisingly lost to Edinburgh but then picked themselves up to record wins against Scarlets, Zebre and Ospreys before losing away to Munster. Their desire to progress to the play-offs showed in the next tranche of matches as Glasgow achieved wins over Zebre and Cardiff on either side of a dramatic 34–34 draw with Leinster in Dublin. Connacht then felt the ambition of Glasgow but the Warriors were given a strong reality check in Swansea, losing to an Ospreys side also very much in the title race.

That reverse in South Wales, however, provided the motivation to emerge from the body repair shop in near pristine condition for their last-round match against title-chasing Ulster at Scotstoun. In the event the Warriors' star players delivered more than enough to secure a comfortable win over the Belfast men, resulting in Glasgow finishing top of the championship table after a desperately tight fight with Munster.

Glasgow and Munster finished level on championship points, but the Scottish side had more wins and thus edged out their Irish rivals. Crucially both Warriors and Munster therefore secured home semi-finals. Ospreys, meanwhile, after failing to gain a bonus point in the final-round match against Connacht, had to settle for third place, just one championship point behind the top two. Making up the quartet of qualifiers was fourth-placed Ulster.

ABOVE The much-missed Munster coach, the late Anthony Foley, during the Guinness Pro12 final in Belfast.

ABOVE Glasgow coach Gregor Townsend's success with the Warriors paved his way to the Scotland job.

So, on to the semi-finals, and Glasgow for a second time in the space of six days would play Ulster at Scotstoun while in Limerick Munster were matched against the Ospreys. The Warriors should have felt confident after their 32–10 win the previous week but instead there was a nervousness apparent in Glasgow's play that suggested the pressure of the occasion was bearing down on the team. Moreover, Ulster looked much more fired-up than they had six days earlier, clearly motivated by the prospect of playing in the final at their home ground, Kingspan, in Belfast, which had been selected by the tournament organisers as the venue for the show-case denouement.

It looked very much as if Glasgow had blown their hopes of a place in the final when they trailed Ulster by 9–14 going into the final few minutes of the match. Flanker Chris Henry and Springbok star Ruan Pienaar had scored what were looking like the winning points for Ulster, Glasgow's response being limited to two penalties from Russell and one long-range kick from Hogg. But with five minutes of the match remaining Russell produced a moment of magic, finding space in the Ulster defence and then spinning out a long overhead pass to winger Van der Merwe, who had the pace and the strength to squeeze over in the corner, levelling the scores at 14–14.

The capacity crowd, which included a large contingent of Ulster supporters, held its collective breath as Russell lined up the touchline conversion. If he was nervous the young fly-half did not show it as he coolly put the ball between the posts to give Glasgow a 16–14 lead, an advantage the Belfast men could not change. When the final whistle sounded, the roar, an outpouring of both relief and celebration, from the home fans was equal in passion to any of the decibels produced at Ibrox or Celtic Park. Glasgow Warriors were in the 2014/15 final and would play against past winners Munster, who in the second of the semi-finals had outgunned the Ospreys.

In the days leading up to the final, the mood was upbeat but tempered by the reality of Glasgow's near misses in the previous two seasons. In 2013 the Warriors reached the semi-final but failed to progress, while a year later the Scotstoun side had achieved their ambition of a place in the final only to be soundly defeated by Leinster. Additionally Glasgow were all too conscious of history suggesting Munster to be big-time title performers.

If these thoughts had permeated the minds of the Glasgow squad then they were manifestly absent in the final at Kingspan in Belfast. As though free to express themselves after the pressure and tension of the semi-final, the Warriors played with power, pace and not a little panache. The leading players rose to the occasion and none more than their charismatic second row Leone Nakarawa.

Not your typical boiler-house man, the athletic Nakarawa – rugby's answer to the Harlem Globetrotters – used all his sevens skills, teasing and mesmerising his opponents with outrageous off-loads, to shred the Munster defence, resulting in a 21–3 lead for the Warriors after just thirty-two minutes from tries by Rob Harley, Van der Merwe and Henry Pyrgos, all converted by Russell.

Munster's pressure before and after the break produced a try from Andrew Smith and a second penalty for Ian Keatley. But Glasgow quickly regained control and when Russell converted his own try it remained only for

LEFT Pete Horne grabs possession of a high ball despite Paddy Butler's challenge.

BELOW Fly-half Finn Russell tackles his opposite number Ian Keatley of Munster during the Pro12 final.

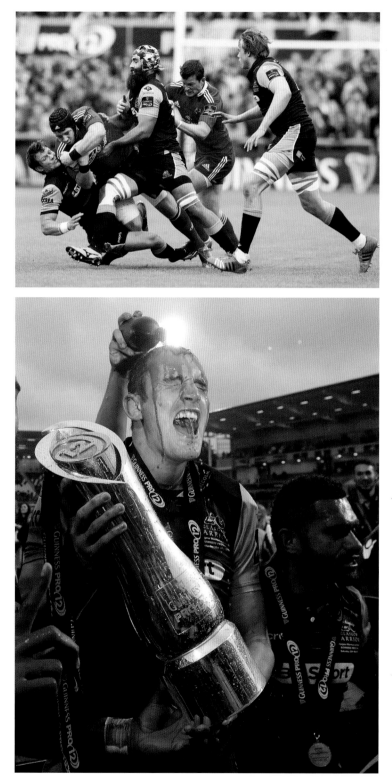

benchman Duncan Weir to add the final points with a penalty goal. Al Kellock, Glasgow's hugely influential lock, was nominated to lift the trophy on behalf of his ecstatic team mates. It was a fitting gesture to the big man in his final game for the Glasgow club which he had so inspired and led over a long career.

Glasgow had achieved a title at last, the first ever by a Scottish club. The immediate dividend was

a confidence lift for Scotland's World Cup squad, who in the autumn of 2015 came desperately close to securing a semi-final place, denied by what many claim (and was confirmed by television replays) was a refereeing blunder by South African official, Craig Joubert, in the dying minutes of the quarter-final against Australia.

If Glasgow's 2015 Pro12 title win further elevated players like Russell and Hogg then so too for their coach Gregor Townsend. The former Scotland and Lions fly-half had succeeded where others had failed, through an insistence on higher fitness levels and handling skills but also allowing his charges to play with a *joie de vivre*. Little wonder then that Townsend was voted coach of the season in the Pro12, an accolade thoroughly deserved and one which undoubtedly was a factor in his ascent to his role with the national team, two years later.

Glasgow's success also kick-started a determination by Murrayfield to raise Edinburgh's game to similar standards. That has now been achieved, reminding east coast fans that the riposte all these years ago to the 'Glasgow's Miles Better' salvo was the pithily crafted ad that spelt out in a Jean Brodie manner: 'Edinburgh's Slightly Superior'. Touché!

A Special Irish Win in Cape Town

PETER O'REILLY

Mention 2016 to any Irish rugby fan and 'Chicago' is probably the first word that he or she will offer. The quest for a Test victory over the All Blacks had taken on an almost mythic quality by the time the teams met at Soldier Field. To have been there when history was created was a privilege. But it wasn't my favourite rugby memory from that year. Work rather got in the way that day. A time difference of minus six hours made for a hellishly tight deadline. Meanwhile the press-box, protected from the elements by double-glazed Perspex, was an atmosphere-free zone. All told, it was a slightly surreal experience.

No, my highlight for that year came a few months earlier, in Cape Town. Ireland made history there, too, beating the Springboks on South African soil for the first time, and doing so in unlikely, dramatic circumstances. That achievement may be overshadowed by Chicago in the history books, but not in my memory. Cape Town was sweet, for a number of reasons.

Maybe my reaction was coloured by memories of reporting on previous tours to South Africa. The locals' rather obvious and outspoken pride in their Springboks can sometimes test your powers of journalistic impartiality and objectivity, shall we say. The 1998 Test series was an ill-tempered affair, with Ireland losing both Tests heavily. Six years later, the situation had changed significantly. The Boks' new coach, Jake White, had picked a raw, inexperienced side. Ireland had just won a Triple Crown. It looked a great opportunity for them. The Boks out-muscled them again, however, and won the series 2–0.

Jump forward twelve years to 2016 – a considerable gap between tours. That's one of the things that made the occasion special, its rarity value. It's over a century since Ireland first played South Africa – in Belfast in 1906, when the Boks won 15–12 – and in that time, Ireland have toured South Arica on only five occasions.

They were not expected to buck a losing trend now, not without several key leaders, all injured –

TOP Full-back Jared Payne of Ireland, scorer of the first try in the match, in action against Adriaan Strauss during the First Test of the series, 11 June 2016.

ABOVE C. J. Stander, right, of Ireland is shown a red card by referee Mathieu Raynal for his challenge on Pat Lambie.

BELOW Conor Murray of Ireland scores his side's second try of the First Test despite the tackle of Lood de Jager.

ABOVE Eben Etzebeth of South Africa steals a lineout from Devin Toner.

LEFT By 2016 Siya Kolisi had become a Springbok regular but did not captain the side until 2018.

Johnny Sexton, Seán O'Brien, Peter O'Mahony, Rob Kearney. 'No one gave us a chance going down there,' Jamie Heaslip said subsequently.

For that first Test, the sense of history was enhanced by the location – Newlands, probably my favourite stadium in world rugby. It's also technically the oldest, given that Lansdowne Road has been refashioned as the Aviva Stadium. South Africa have stopped using it for Tests, as it is beginning to show signs of its age. To squeeze into the press box, high up in the Railway Stand, with its ancient fixtures and fittings, is to be transported back to the 1950s. Get in there early if you want to be sure of a power-point. Don't rely on the stadium wifi.

And yet for atmosphere, the old stadium is hard to beat. A lot of it is to do with the stunningly dramatic backdrop of Table Mountain, which looms over the ground, even as evening draws in and the floodlights come on. But it's also the enclosed nature of the stadium, which makes it one of the noisier rugby cauldrons.

The patrons were in especially noisy form that Saturday in June, as they'd been denied the chance to see their favourite team in action for over six months. This was the Boks' first outing since the Rugby World Cup in England, when they'd been pipped by two points in the semi-final by the eventual champions, New Zealand. It was also the first Test under a new coach, Allister Coetzee, adding another layer of intrigue.

The locals were at their noisiest and rowdiest in the twenty-second minute – a pivotal moment in the game and one that made Ireland's eventual victory all the more remarkable. For that was when C. J. Stander was sent off by French referee Mathieu Raynal for what was an unfortunate accident. As Lambie shaped to launch a

ABOVE Faf de Klerk of South Africa touches down safely, ahead of Paddy Jackson of Ireland.

RIGHT Jamie Heaslip is tackled by Frans Malherbe and Tendai Mtawarira (1).

bomb from just inside half-way, Stander jumped to block but only succeeded in catching his opponent flush on the jaw with his hip. It was hard to argue that Stander had intended to do his opponent harm. But Lambie was out cold, albeit briefly, and this surely informed Raynal's decision.

You had sympathy for Lambie, whose game was over, but also for Stander. This game had been on his radar for months – a return to the country of his birth, at a stadium only a couple of hours' drive from the family home, where he had captained the Baby Boks only a few years previously before becoming disillusioned at his lack of opportunity and heading to Munster as a 'project' player.

A few months before the tour, in the middle of what was his first Six Nations, Stander had told me of his desire to play against the Springboks – to make a point to a few people who'd said that he was too small for international rugby but also to perform for his grandfather, Frederick, who was hoping to be at Newlands. 'If I get selected, it would be massive,' Stander said. 'It's a big drive for me. Granddad played eighthman [number 8] for our local club, and taught me a lot about the game – how to play, how to work your arse off. He's a Springboks supporter and you can't ever change that but he will still support me. He just wants to see me play at the highest level I can.'

Frederick was there that day, so too Stander's parents and other members of the family. How dreadful to see their boy sent from the field, booed by some of the locals. Typically, Stander's first concern was for Lambie, who reassured him there was no ill-feeling. Stander's one-match ban meant that he was available to play the

TIME SOUTH AFRICA 20
03:49 IRELAND 23

TOP Paddy Jackson kicks a penalty to put his side six points ahead late in the First Test, completing Ireland's 26–20 victory.

third and final Test of the series, in Port Elizabeth, where South Africa's win saw them take the series 2–1.

Back in Cape Town, Ireland's immediate concern was with protecting the lead they had built through Jared Payne's early try. It was hard work, made even harder when Robbie Henshaw was binned for a high tackle on Lambie's replacement, Elton Jantjies, who helped set up Lwazi Mvovo with an equalising try.

The sides were level at 13–13 by the break. We expected South Africa's extra man to count, especially given the quality they had in the pack – eight of their forwards that day would feature the day they captured the 2019 Rugby World Cup in Yokohama.

But Ireland's coach Joe Schmidt had reasons for optimism. This was Andy Farrell's first Test as defence coach and there was an unmistakable energy in the way they went about sawing down the Boks. The likes of Henshaw, Payne and Heaslip were leading by example, while a couple of young Ulstermen were also stepping forward – Luke Marshall was highly aggressive in midfield, while Paddy Jackson brought composure, typified by his forty-metre drop-goal.

It helped Jackson that Conor Murray was on top of his game at scrum-half. He imprinted his personality on the game two minutes into the second half, darting under Eben Etzebeth's attempted tackle for Ireland's second try. Jackson converted – he would miss just one kick from six shots at goal, a penalty that rebounded off the post early in the third quarter. But Ireland were still three points clear at that stage, which became ten in the sixty-eighth minute, thanks to a Jackson penalty. They were still defending ferociously, too.

Then the game was turned on its head once more when Pieter-Steph du Toit intercepted Jackson's pass on the Irish 22 and sprinted over, setting up a fantastically tense end-game.

A Springboks' steal was possible right until the final play, when J. P. Pietersen was bundled into touch in the left corner by a welcoming party of Henshaw, Payne, Jackson and Rhys Ruddock. It was appropriate that Ireland's defence should have the final say for it was the foundation for victory.

'I thought it was an incredible collective effort,' Schmidt said afterwards. 'The nine minutes before half-time when we were down to 13 players, to just put them out in the corner, just to scramble and work as hard as the players did to keep them out, was exceptional. There was almost a direct repeat at the end of the second half again. To their attacking left-hand corner, we managed to scramble across and three or four players turned up to avoid the try being scored. The players can be incredibly proud of the effort they put in.'

We toasted them in Cape Town that night.

The Year of Rugby's Ultimate Draw

MILES HARRISON

2016–2017

Many moons ago, my English teacher talked the class through Rudyard Kipling's 'If' and, inevitably, we discussed the 'triumph and disaster' bit: 'And treat those two impostors just the same.' The discussion developed into how, as members of school teams, we should react to winning and losing. Of course, our teacher encouraged us to accept those outcomes with equal grace and humility and it is fair to say we had seen his important lesson coming. However, what he said next made us sit up and take note. Reactions to victory and defeat were easy, he professed, it is how you conduct yourself in the face of a draw that shows your true character. We wanted to hear more.

This was my teacher's argument. Winning clearly gives a glow of satisfaction but, as long as the individual manages to keep their reaction in reasonable check, then they are likely to keep their good character intact as well. Defeat also comes with a moment of clear realisation as the scoreboard rarely lies. It is here that the individual has little choice but to doff the cap to their opponent and say 'well done'. The real issue arises with a draw, as this is when the sportsperson can allow into their mind a thousand regrets, those inches that, had they gone the other way, could have taken them to victory. If you permit these thoughts to take over, the door is opened to merely focussing on yourself and, perhaps, inviting in other 'impostors' such as arrogance, petulance and the like. My teacher concluded that, in the aftermath of a draw, you could see truly inside the sporting soul as, at this point, the magnanimous handshake and knowing look mean so much more. When honours are even, it is imperative to do the honourable thing.

As with all lessons at school, some you take on board and some you don't. However, this view of sport and,

> **ABOVE** Elliot Daly is denied a try by a superb last-moment tackle from Israel Dagg, First Test.

I suppose life, made a big impression on the young me. Little did I know back then, though, how perfectly I would see the lesson played out in all its shining glory on a famous rugby day: Saturday 8 July 2017, the never to be forgotten Third Test between the British and

ABOVE Seán O'Brien of the Lions dives over for his team's first try, First Test, Eden Park, 24 June 2017.

BELOW Hooker Codie Taylor scored the first try of the match but lost out here in the air to Anthony Watson.

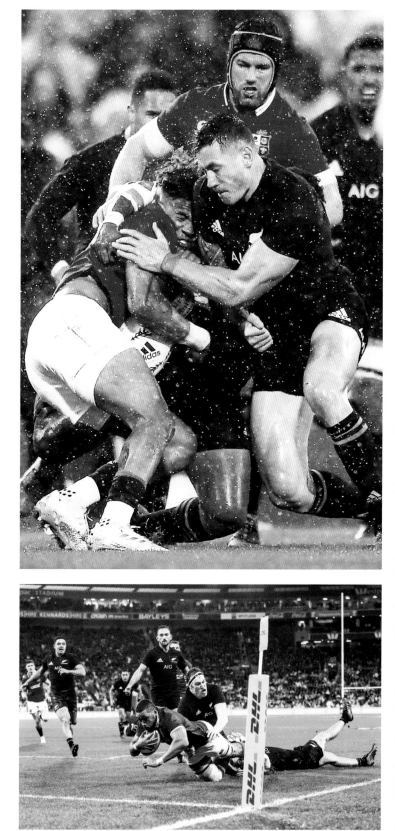

Irish Lions and New Zealand at Eden Park.

It was my sixth Lions' tour behind the microphone for Sky Sports and the tour that simply had to deliver. The depth of that feeling went all the way back to 2005, the Lions' previous trip to New Zealand which, for somebody who had fallen in love with rugby in the early seventies long before my teacher quoted Kipling to me, was meant to be the pinnacle of my broadcasting career. The Lions in New Zealand, it doesn't get any bigger, or so I thought. The truth though is that, when events fall so cataclysmically short of expectation, the disappointment doesn't come any bigger either. Don't get me totally wrong because, off the field, 2005 was a ball as New Zealand hosted in that friendly camper-van sort of way, a country that puts its guests totally at ease. But, on the field, the Lions never fired a shot and the gulf between the two sides ultimately made for a sporting non-event.

So, 2017 had to be different. The early signs were that it would be. The Blues and the Highlanders gave the Lions clear warnings, not that those salvos are particularly required when touring New Zealand, but the Lions' response was a good one. The great Crusaders were beaten and then so too were the Maori All Blacks and the Chiefs. By the time we got to the week before the First Test, you felt the Lions were almost where they needed to be. On the modern-day Lions tour, it is a crazy race against time to get to this point of readiness but these Lions had just about done it.

What followed was a classic series full of drama and brilliant rugby. Seán O'Brien's try in the First Test will go down as one of the greatest ever Lions' scores; indeed, for many, it might even be the greatest. The Second Test's 'moment' centred on something a whole lot more negative, the sending-off of Sonny Bill Williams. That, and the appallingly wet night in Wellington, certainly played into the Lions' paws but the way they held their nerve to come through as victors marked this team out as a special group.

All-square then and, when we woke on the morning of the Third Test, little did we know that it would still be all-square by the time we made our weary ways to bed when night turned into the morning after. In the interim, those lucky enough to be there had witnessed as compelling an end to a game and a series as you could ever imagine. Owen Farrell's late penalty-goal and, once again, his inner steel to produce for his team when it mattered most, seemed to have levelled things for good. Yet, from the restart, New Zealand were awarded a penalty of their own and, suddenly, all seemed lost for the Lions. However, referee Romain Poite remarkably reversed his decision and awarded a scrum. The man who had given away the 'penalty that never was', Lions' hooker, Ken Owens, waited, arms outstretched, for his colleagues to join him in the front-row to link

RIGHT Jordie Barrett scores his side's second try during the Third Test.

BELOW Alun Wyn Jones of the Lions is felled by Jerome Kaino during the Third Test. Maro Itoje arrives in support.

together hurriedly as if he feared the referee was about to change his mind again. In the little time available, both sides threw everything they had at trying to engineer a winning score but couldn't do it.

And, when the final whistle went, with the scores still level at 15-all, nobody knew quite how to react. The Lions' head coach, a Kiwi himself of course, Warren Gatland, went down to the pitch to shake the hand of his counterpart, Steve Hansen, who famously described the dramatic finish as 'a bit like kissing your sister'. The players shared their coaches' unease and did not know quite what to do with themselves either. But, crucially, the positive sporting tone that had been set by the captains all the way through the series bore fruit in that moment of controversy at the end of this epic contest. Lions' skipper, Sam Warburton's panic at the initial penalty award admirably did not turn into heated protestations. New Zealand captain, Kieran Read, having seen the referee backtrack, was aghast at what was happening in front of his eyes but commendably restricted his pleas to a minimum. Both men had not only kept their cool but even exchanged a knowing chuckle. It was a lesson in how to show respect to your opponent, the officials and the game and all the more impressive given the scale of what hangs on the result of a Lions tour both for the host and the visitor.

The players then gathered to pose for the photograph that will go down in the history of the game, even sport, as one of the great post-series podium shots. The trophy was shared by the skippers and then Lions and

All Blacks, red and black, side by side, smile by smile, shared the hurt of not achieving their ultimate goal too. They had faced their thousand regrets and, shoulder to shoulder, they produced the picture that made sure that the bigger picture had been kept in mind. Without everybody necessarily knowing it at the time, it was, for the sporting soul a perfect end – the draw, true test of sporting character.

LEFT Owen Farrell of the Lions celebrates after kicking a long-range penalty to level the scores at 12–12 during the Third Test.

BELOW Opposing captains Kieran Read of the All Blacks and Sam Warburton of the Lions lift the trophy at the end of the drawn series.

St Patrick's Day Well Celebrated

RUAIDHRI O'CONNOR

The snow fell quickly over south-west London, but the players on the Twickenham turf were impervious to the cold. Up in the stands, shivering fans lingered to savour the moment through chattering teeth. Days like this don't come around too often. In truth, 2018 was a succession of great moments for Irish rugby but to win a Grand Slam away to England on St Patrick's Day with perhaps the most complete away performance ever produced by an Irish team will go down as an era-defining match.

For an entire generation of Irish followers, Twickenham is a forbidding place packed with bad memories. When the game goes against the visiting team, things can get ugly, as Andy Farrell and his men found out in 2020. That's why every one of the fourteen Irish wins at Headquarters is remembered in its own way. None hold the same place as this one.

It was a year like no other for the game in Ireland, the zenith of the tenure of Ireland's most successful coach, Joe Schmidt, and the peak of a team that was building steadily towards this moment. The subsequent fall-off in the World Cup year of 2019 took some sheen off the achievements, but a calendar year that saw Schmidt's side lose just once while claiming a Six Nations clean-sweep, a 2–1 series win over Australia and a historic first win over the All Blacks in Dublin and ended with them dominating the World Rugby Awards stands alone as an achievement. On that awards night in Monaco, the team's inspirational leader Johnny Sexton was crowned World Player of the Year, their coach picked up the Coach of the Year gong and the team were named Team of the Year.

It started and finished with outrageous sporting moments that transcended Irish life and will be discussed for generations. The Grand Slam was on the rocks in Paris before the team somehow put together a forty-four-phase move that ended with Sexton nailing a clutch drop-goal to steal the game from the French in injury time. That gave them momentum and they rolled through the Championship. Young winger Jacob

TOP How it started. Jonathan Sexton lands the last-seconds long-range drop goal to win the opening match against France.

ABOVE Garry Ringrose touches down for the first St Patrick's Day try.

RIGHT Rob Kearney manages to disrupt Anthony Watson's catch of a high ball.

Stockdale set a record for tries scored on his debut season as they proved too strong for Wales, Scotland and Italy at home before they travelled to London to take on Eddie Jones's men, who had won the title the two previous seasons.

Ireland had denied England a Grand Slam in Dublin a year previously, but the English could do nothing to stop the green wave on home soil. On a bitterly cold afternoon, Ireland produced a near-perfect performance laced with physical venom with their game-plan carried out with precision.

Tries from Garry Ringrose and Stockdale book-ended the half, but it was C. J. Stander's score that summed up the point this team had got to in their development. Tighthead prop Tadhg Furlong was the architect, releasing Bundee Aki with a cleverly

disguised pass. The Connacht centre burst through a gap and had the presence of mind to find his number 8 on the inside shoulder. The powerful South African did the rest. Stockdale's score in first-half injury time

gave his team an unassailable lead and Jonny May's consolation try put some sheen on a 24–15 defeat for the home team.

'It was absolutely Baltic, not what you associate with the middle of March,' full-back Rob Kearney recalled. 'Even still to this day talking to family and friends, people who were there said it was the coldest they had ever been. But, when you're getting into the last fifteen or twenty minutes, you've won a Grand Slam, you don't really care too much about the cold. When you're doing the lap of honour you're going to milk every moment of it. But there was snow coming down during the first half, looking at Jacob Stockdale's try with the clock in the red.'

Scrum-half Conor Murray remembers the team achieving a rare level of focus as they set out to finish the job. 'That whole week, our attitude and our mindset were really good. We knew we had to go to Twickenham and perform, not to take risks or chances but to go after the game and attack the game,' the scrum-half said. 'I thought we did that really well. It was one of our best performances defensively. That really helped overall. Before half-time, our decision to run a "D" play – I think Jacob scored with a chip and chase – having the willingness to go and chase that, a lot of teams might have waited to the 40 minutes and kicked it out. That day, that season, we backed ourselves, which was fantastic.'

ABOVE LEFT Irish defence. Elliot Daly is held by Jacob Stockdale (*left*) and flanker Dan Leavy (*right*).

LEFT C. J. Stander scores Ireland's second try despite the tackle of England flanker James Haskell.

Understandably, given the weather, many fans had left the arena when Rory Best lifted the trophy to the sky but it meant the players could connect with family members and fans as they slowly made their way around the pitch to soak up the moment.

They rumbled on from there: many of the team were involved when Leinster picked up a Heineken Champions Cup in Bilbao and added the Guinness Pro14 in Dublin two weeks later.

Ireland then went to Australia and, while they lost the First Test in Brisbane, they rebounded to win in Melbourne and Sydney. On they rolled to November and the arrival of the All Blacks.

Ireland had beaten the world champions in Chicago in 2016, but they'd never done it on home soil and, so, their 16–9 victory in Dublin was cherished by the 53,000 people there to witness it.

Again, Stockdale scored the all-important try off another Schmidt-designed pre-planned move. Again, Sexton drove the team around and Peter O'Mahony produced his greatest performance. When Brodie Retallick knocked on in injury time as the men in black pushed for a try to level matters, the Aviva Stadium erupted like never before and grown men wept at a sight they never thought they'd see.

Even two years on, it is difficult to reconcile the standards Ireland reached during that unforgettable year. Lockdown afforded a chance to catch up on the footage and take stock of an achievement that will live long in the memory of Irish rugby. Life has moved on. England are now Europe's dominant force and for Ireland everything is a bit of a struggle.

It's a reminder that those heights, when you hit them, must be enjoyed and savoured. On that freezing cold day in Twickenham beneath the slate-grey skies, a team hit the peak of its powers and blew their oldest rivals away to secure a prize they'd only won twice in their history. Whatever came after that, nobody could take it away from them.

They'll always have St Patrick's Day, 2018.

ABOVE Second row James Ryan (*left*) and flanker Dan Leavy celebrate with the Championship and Triple Crown trophies.

The Finest Calcutta Cup Game of All

CHRIS JONES

England fans travelled to Twickenham on 16 March 2019 dreaming of another Six Nations title; they left shell-shocked after one of the most bizarre and outright brilliant games of rugby ever played in this famous old tournament.

Ahead of the Calcutta Cup, all eyes were on Cardiff. A win for Ireland would have kept alive England's hopes of nicking the trophy, which would have been a significant psychological boost in Rugby World Cup year. But Wales's crushing display, a victory at a canter, sealed their Grand Slam. News trickled through to the England and Scotland players in their warm-up that the destiny of the title was decided, and at the same time the atmosphere in the bars around Twickenham instantly flattened. Was the Calcutta Cup now set to be a desperate anti-climax?

As I prepared for the BBC Radio commentary, with former England and Scotland captains Matt Dawson and Andy Nicol alongside me, and Paul Grayson on the touchline, there was a lingering sense that the real story was 150 miles away on the streets of Cardiff. St Mary Street would be jumping. Had we gone to the wrong game? A windy and damp afternoon didn't help build the occasion, especially when the froth from punters' beer rained down on the commentary box from the upper tier, leaving flecks of Guinness all over the team-sheets.

With conditions drying up just in time for kick-off, England stormed out of the blocks, seemingly both angry and liberated, with Jack Nowell scooting over after sixty-six seconds. Eddie Jones's men then came again, with Tom Curry scoring from a rolling maul, Joe Launchbury crossed after Kyle Sinckler scythed clear, before Henry Slade gave a cheeky flick for Jonny May to wrap up the try bonus point under half an hour. There was confidence bordering on arrogance, as England popped open the champagne.

The home side were rampant, 31–0 up in a place Scotland hadn't won since 1983. How many would

> **BELOW & OPPOSITE** It could hardly be going better for England. Try no. 2 by Tom Curry (*below*); no. 3 by Joe Launchbury (*top right*); and no. 4 from Jonny May (*right*). Add in four conversions and a penalty from Owen Farrell: 31–0 and not even half an hour gone.

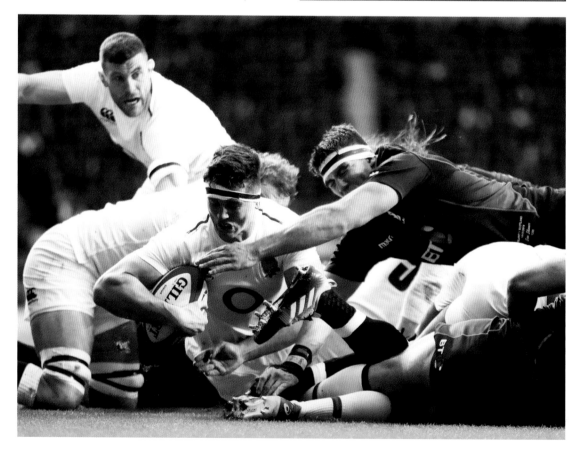

England go on to win by? 50 points? 60? Maybe even more? In 2017, it had finished 61–21 at Twickenham; after 29 minutes this time, Scottish supporters might have settled for that. 'England are playing a different game to Scotland,' said Grayson. 'Scotland are half-asleep.'

It seemed like party time at Twickenham. 'This is bad. It could get horrendous,' Nicol added.

With Eddie Jones regaining his mojo after a difficult 2018, England had flexed their muscles already in the tournament, dispatching Ireland so impressively in Dublin and crushing the French, with only a second-half capitulation in Wales denying them from a shot at a Slam. With their dynamic, powerful forwards and clever and sharp backs, England were establishing them-selves as World Cup contenders. A bullying thrashing of the hapless Scots looked inevitable as half-time approached, especially with Gregor Townsend's side limping to the final weekend, injury-ravaged and with just a solitary win against Italy to show for 2019.

With five minutes of the first forty to go, and England pressing again in the Scotland half, captain Owen Farrell went to chip only to be charged down by opposite skipper Stuart McInally. The hooker gathered brilliantly and galloped over half-way; remark-

ably, he held off both Farrell and the rapid May to score next to the posts; respite for the Scots at the break, but surely nothing more. 'That's good for the game,' mused Dawson prophetically.

'You would not have bet a pound on him to score with Jonny May on his shoulder,' said Grayson. 'An extraordinary score.'

'I'm going to pick on the positives . . . Scotland have won the last five minutes!' laughed Nicol, leaning on gallows' humour in a time of crisis.

While we scoffed some half-time biscuits, harsh words were being spoken below us in the Twickenham tunnel. Fly-half Finn Russell was later to reveal how he was involved in a stand-off with another stand-off, as he and Townsend – himself a former 10 in Russell's image – clashed over tactics.

'I would love to have heard what Gregor Townsend said in that changing room,' remarked Nicol at the start of the second half. Let's see if anything changes. It has to, because that was so poor in the first half. There could be deep scars here that you might not recover from. They have to restore some pride in the second half.'

Whatever was said, Scotland started the second half like a train, finally stringing some phases together. Russell's beautiful inside ball found centre Sam Johnson, who linked with scrum-half Ali Price, before quick recycled ball saw wing Darcy Graham dance over. 'This could be the greatest of all comebacks,' quipped Nicol, surely more in hope than expectation.

But seconds later, the quick-witted Price was at it again, chipping for himself from inside his own half before having the awareness to feed the marauding number 8 Magnus Bradbury, who stormed over for Scotland's third, as the visiting fans – hitherto subdued – started to stir.

31–19, as we began to commentate on our feet rather than from our seats. 'The battle of the coaches at half-time is being won by Gregor Townsend,' said Dawson. 'Eddie Jones has been left wanting at half-time again, like he was in Cardiff.'

Body language transformed, Scotland started to rock England back on the gain-line, although a burst from Manu Tuilagi took England deep into opposition territory and checked Scottish optimism. But Scotland survived, and edged back into the English half as we ticked towards the hour mark. 'One more score and Scotland are right back in it,' added Grayson.

Townsend made five changes, including the experienced Greig Laidlaw for the effervescent Price. Scottish tails were up as Laidlaw linked with another replacement, Chris Harris, before a genius pass from the buoyant Russell – not quite the vintage of his legendary ball in the same fixture the previous year, but not far off – found Sean Maitland over from his wing, and he gave it to Graham, who skinned Elliot Daly to dot down.

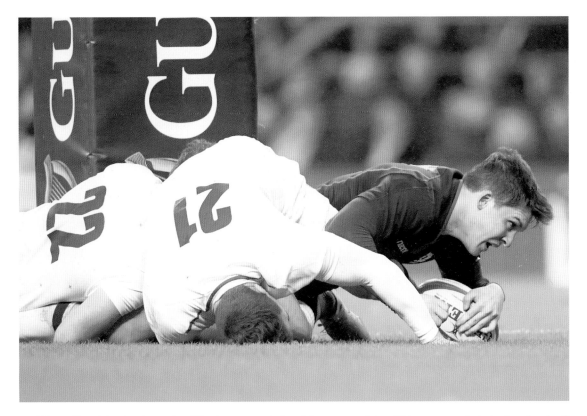

Three Scottish tries in under 10 minutes, and the visitors moved to within seven points, to the shock of Twickenham and Jones, who cut a bemused figure just below us in the coaching box. Following that score, the noise shot up around the famous old ground, as the Scotland supporters found their voices and the English started to implore their team to restore normality. But Russell was far from finished, picking off the pass of the flustered Farrell – with a little juggle, apt for a man performing the role of the circus-master – before racing in from fifty metres.

'I am not believing what I am seeing at the moment!' gasped Nicol. 'Russell read the play beautifully. This is truly stunning.'

Laidlaw popped over the conversion to tie the scores. 'Truly extraordinary,' reflected Grayson from his touchline position.

'I've found a lot of Scottish friends!' said Dawson as the texts started to flood in.

England's composure and leadership were being seriously questioned, even more so when Graham was checked by Farrell's shoulder with fourteen minutes left. Penalty Scotland, and a chance to take the lead. On the edge of his range, Laidlaw missed, and Twickenham breathed again.

Jones had seen enough, and did the unthinkable, hooking the frustrated Farrell for George Ford, who took over the captaincy for good measure as the rain again started to swirl around us. 'Home and away means nothing now,' said Dawson.

Five minutes left, and England again coughed up possession, allowing Scotland to burst to within forty metres. Russell – a good ten minutes since producing a moment of magic – pulled another rabbit out of the hat, miraculously putting Johnson through while looking in the opposite direction, sending Tuilagi into a different postcode in the process. Johnson did the rest, and there was plenty to do, finishing magnificently past Nowell and Daly. Scotland, impossibly, were seven points clear.

'The Scottish bench have just gone ballistic. I've not seen anything like it!' said Dawson.

'If that is the try to win the game – the most bonkers game I have ever watched quite frankly – then it is fitting! Not a single Scottish player was alive when Scotland last won at Twickenham,' added an ecstatic Nicol.

'Russell was almost looking directly at me,' explained Grayson, who was level with the play. 'Sensational.'

Three minutes left, and Scotland had possession in their own half. Two and a half minutes to go, and England won it on the floor, only for Ellis Genge to be stripped by Russell, who proceeded to pin England back on their own 22. Ninety seconds left. Game over, surely.

England had to go eighty metres in eighty seconds, a challenge Ford took on. Clever work from the replacement fly-half released Tom Curry, as England worked up to half-way, before May was stranded on the left touchline. But the winger somehow stayed infield, ducking under the challenges of Adam Hastings and Hamish Watson to keep the ball alive – a decisive piece of play, which Scottish players and fans were to rue.

With the clock in the red, a penalty to England, as for the first time in the second half the Scots looked weary. Laidlaw gesticulated angrily; Scotland just needed to keep their discipline. Ford took the hosts to within ten metres. Nicol smacked the table.

George Kruis claimed the line-out, with the Scottish bench on their feet ready to invade the pitch. But Nowell scampered close, so did replacement Ben Te'o, as Scotland conceded one penalty, then another. Nowell again went to within inches, then Kruis, before replacement scrum-half Ben Spencer fed Genge, the prop flicking it on brilliantly to the superb Ford, who glided under the posts to save the game, and break Scottish hearts.

'I don't know what to say,' reflected an exhausted Nicol. 'To be disappointed with a draw when you've been 31–0 down . . . but they got themselves in a winning position. I genuinely don't know how to feel.'

'I have never experienced an England side lose such a lead,' said England's World Cup winning scrum-half Matt Dawson. 'It's extremely frustrating.'

Dawson's frustration was shared by head coach Jones, who seemed at a loss to explain the capitulation during his post-match media duties, while for Townsend it was a performance that saved his side's Championship, albeit with a lingering sense of what might have been; the first win since 1983 and all that. Scotland's two-try hero, wing Darcy Graham told us it came down to putting some pride back in the shirts after an 'embarrassing' first half.

Sloping out of Twickenham that evening, it was clear there have been Calcutta Cup matches that have meant more in the context of the tournament: 1990 at Murrayfield for example. But in terms of drama, unpredictability, and sheer rugby madness, it surely won't get better than this.

Body language. (*Above left*) Owen Farrell sits apart from his glum team-mates, a picture of misery and confusion. But (*left*) Ben Te'o couldn't be more delighted by George Ford's last seconds try with the simple equalising conversion to come.

Japan's Wonderful World Cup

ALASTAIR EYKYN

This was the never-ending season, the rugby equivalent of cricket's Timeless Test. Little did we know as the Rugby World Cup kicked off in Tokyo in mid-September 2019, of the disrupted, pot-holed path ahead. The sport's showpiece had to endure an enormously damaging natural disaster, in order to crown new World Champions. But, as it turned out, Typhoon Hagibis in Japan was a portent of the worldwide havoc ahead, in the form of Covid-19. The planet was ravaged, and rugby suffered, just as everyone suffered.

'Japan 2019' broke new ground. The first Rugby World Cup to be held in Asia, the tournament spread the gospel of the oval ball to a whole new audience. The competition galvanised previously untapped support across the continent, and a collective worldwide TV audience of up to one billion people helped draw new supporters, and grow new sporting heroes. Those of us lucky enough to be there can testify to the impact on the beautiful country of Japan, and to that special sense of occasion that is only felt at global events that engender a broad outlook, beyond conventional boundaries.

Rugby fans from all over the globe swept in to Japan, to experience a whole new culture. They wandered dazed and confused through the Tokyo subway, scratched their heads in wonder at the stunning array of local delicacies, soaked up both the staggering beauty of the Japanese countryside, and the dynamism and energy of their kaleidoscopic cities. They were indebted to the thousands of locals who guided them through it with a patience, politeness and grace that would be hard to match.

As for the rugby itself, it began with an emotional opening night in Tokyo. A fairytale hat-trick from Kotaro Matsushima helped a nervous host nation topple the Russians, and the Brave Blossoms were on their way. Once they had learned to channel the weight of expectation from their adoring fans, the Japanese went on to play a thrilling brand of rugby that took them into the history books.

The tournament was set alight by the Japanese claiming their first major scalp. It proved to be one of the greatest World Cup shocks, as they powered their way to victory over hot favourites Ireland in Shizuoka. Every tackle, every carry and every turn-over was cheered on by a cacophonous home crowd who sensed that their moment had arrived. On each of the seven occasions that they had met before, Japan had lost by a margin of

Emotions. (*Left*) Rikiya Matsuda and Isileli Nakajima (*left*) celebrate Japan's victory over Ireland; (*right*) Tomas Lavanini of Argentina realises how much damage his red card has done to his team in the pool game with England; (*below right*) Kyle Sinckler of England relishes every step of his quarter-final try against Australia.

more than thirty points. This time, their attacking game plan was unrelenting.

Despite conceding tries to Garry Ringrose and Rob Kearney before the break, Yu Tamura's goal-kicking kept the Brave Blossoms in touch on the scoreboard. Their off-loading and fast-paced approach was winning over supporters everywhere, and on the hour mark their talisman Kenki Fukuoka flew over in the corner for the crucial try. Tamura's late penalty sealed an enormously significant win, the like of which Japan had not experienced since Brighton in 2015 and that extra-ordinary performance that toppled the mighty Springboks.

Jamie Joseph's team had a taste for success, at this point, not to mention that most precious of sporting commodities, momentum. It saw them through against Samoa, and left a tantalisingly poised showdown with Scotland, who had recovered well from their opening loss to Ireland, in their final match in the pool. It was then that Mother Nature intervened.

No one will ever forget the way the Japanese responded to Typhoon Hagibis. Within twenty-four hours of one of the most destructive storms ever to strike the country, they rallied in defiance, to stage a sporting occasion that will live forever in the memory. Operational staff slept on site at the Yokohama International Stadium, and were up at 4 a.m. assessing the damage, planning the recovery. Men and women whose homes and families were affected by the flooding, the landslides and the extensive damage brought to bear by the typhoon, bound together and worked tirelessly to ensure a rugby match took place.

Their team rode the powerful wave of emotion that tumbled down from the stands that night, and delivered a virtuoso performance that stopped the Scots in their tracks, and lifted the spirits of every rugby fan, regardless of nationality. Once more it was Kenki Fukuoka who tore the heart out of the Scotland challenge; his two tries took Japan into the last eight from Pool A. It was a landmark moment; the first time an Asian side had reached the knock-out stages of the Rugby World Cup.

Elsewhere, the big beasts quietly moved into position. New Zealand struck the first blow, in seeing off South Africa in their seismic opening match of the pool. Early tries from George Bridge and Scott Barrett put the All Blacks out of reach, and the Springboks could not reel them in. Both worked their way into the quarter-finals from Pool B.

In Pool C, England and France picked a way through, as the Pumas faltered. The French undid Argentina at the death, thanks to a dramatic late drop-goal from Camille Lopez. Against England, the Argentinians shot

Taking a stand. (*Above*) England confront the *haka* before their semi-final win over New Zealand; (*left*) Welsh players stand alone and bereft in the moment of their semi-final defeat to South Africa.

themselves in the foot as Tomas Lavanini was sent off in the first half, and Eddie Jones's men made short work of the remaining fourteen men.

Of them all, the least predictable was Pool D, where the Fijians were tipped to create havoc. Sadly for the neutral, their team of all-stars fluffed their lines. They lost their opener to Australia in Sapporo, and then most memorably to little-fancied Uruguay in Kamaishi – a city that had suffered untold damage from an earthquake in 2011, and a deadly tsunami that followed. As the locals toasted the symbolism of their recovery from one of Japan's darkest days, South American tears flowed freely as the part-timers celebrated their first World Cup victory since 2003. The pivotal match in the pool took place in Tokyo, where Wales held out for a narrow 29–25 win over the Wallabies, despite having led 23–8 at the break. Josh Adams then scored a hat-trick, as Wales beat Fiji in Oita, meaning Warren Gatland's men finished top of the pile.

The first two quarter-finals were one-sided. Jonny May scored twice as England thumped Australia, and prompted the resignation of Michael Cheika as head coach. New Zealand scored seven tries against Ireland, confirming their tag as favourites to defend their crown. Progress for the French was harder to come by; ill-discipline condemned them, as Sébastien Vahaamahina was sent off for a mindless elbow to the face of Aaron Wainwright. They led the Welsh 19–10 at the time, but surrendered their advantage, and a late try from Ross Moriarty led Wales into the semi-final. The quarter-finals also proved the end of the line for the sensational Japanese, as the Brave Blossoms ran into a South African juggernaut, intent on overpowering anything that got in their way.

The semi-finals were magnificent contests. Inspired by a V-shaped response to the *haka*, England produced a performance that many seasoned campaigners considered to be their best ever in international rugby. They overturned the vaunted All Blacks with an indomitable spirit, and a staggering back-row display in which youngsters Sam Underhill and Tom Curry touched new heights. With an early Manu Tuilagi try, and the deadly kicking of George Ford, England dethroned the defending champions. In the other semi-final, South Africa edged out the Welsh by the narrowest of margins. Handré Pollard never missed from the tee, and Damian de Allende's try proved critical.

The Rugby World Cup final was a cagey affair. England were jittery and error-strewn; South Africa inspired and clinical. The match only burst into life after an hour, as Makazole Mapimpi and Cheslin Kolbe applied the gloss to a belligerent Springbok performance. To witness Siya Kolisi lift the trophy as the first black South African captain was to understand the enormous significance of sport's ability to unify. Twenty-four years on from the moment that brought the Rainbow Nation together, and wearing the same iconic number 6 shirt worn by both François Pienaar and Nelson Mandela, the boy from a township raised the William Webb Ellis Cup high into the air.

The symbolism was unmissable, the captain's words inspirational: 'We have so many problems in our country but to have a team like this . . . we come from different backgrounds, different races and we came together with one goal and we wanted to achieve it. I really hope we have done that for South Africa, to show that we can pull together if we want to achieve something. We love you, South Africa, and we can achieve anything if we work together as one.'

RIGHT Cheslin Kolbe's try rounds off South Africa's win in the final. Anthony Watson realises the dream has gone.

BELOW Siya Kolisi celebrates with his wife and family during a Springbok victory parade in Cape Town.